# *The Convection Oven Cookbook*

# Contents

# Introduction

## Convection Cooking

In a convection oven, a fan circulates hot air around the food and evenly distributes it throughout the oven cavity. The circulating air uniformly heats the food, producing a crisp, brown exterior. Conventional baking and roasting temperatures may need to be reduced by 25°F when convection cooking. Refer to individual charts and recipes for best baking temperatures. See the Use and Care Guide for design/feature information concerning your particular oven model.

Circulating air prevents heat from collecting at the top of the oven and creates a more uniform oven temperature.

## Convection Techniques

**Many of the techniques used in conventional cooking are also important when cooking by convection. Following these recommendations will assure exceptional baking results.**

The same cookware and utensils that are normally used when conventionally baking can also be used in convection ovens. For best results, however, use shiny, aluminum utensils.

Dark or matte finish utensils will produce darker browning on food surfaces.

Heat-resistant paper and plastic containers that manufacturers recommend for use in conventional ovens can be used in convection ovens. Plastic cooking utensils that are heat resistant to temperatures of 400°F are also suitable.

Use a pan with low sides whenever possible. A shallow pan allows air to circulate around the food more efficiently.

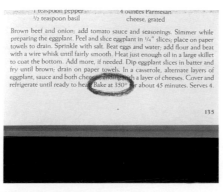

As a general rule, reduce conventional baking temperatures by 25°F.

Remember, oven walls, shelves and cooking utensils do get hot during convection cooking. Always use dry oven mitts when removing utensils from the oven.

# *Introduction*

## *Convection Results*

**Any food that can be cooked in a conventional oven, cooks beautifully in a convection oven. In fact, professional chefs choose convection ovens for consistently superior baking and roasting results.**

Convection roasting is ideal for meats. Moisture and flavor are sealed in quickly as circulating hot air browns the surface.

Chicken and other poultry develop crisp golden skin but stay juicy and tender.

Casseroles may bake in less time or at a lower temperature than in a conventional oven.

Pies baked in a convection oven are evenly browned, tender and flaky.

The convection oven's uniform temperature helps keep airy foods, such as cream puffs, high and light.

Breads baked in the convection oven have consistent texture and evenly browned crusts.

## Adapting Recipes for Convection Cooking

1. As a general rule to follow when converting recipes for convection baking, reduce baking temperatures by 25°F. Exceptions are roasts, layer cakes, yeast breads and two-crust pies (see below).
2. Cook times may be reduced, as well. Some foods may actually cook in ¼ to ⅓ less time in the convection oven (see chart).
3. Preheating the oven is usually not necessary. However, preheating may be desirable for foods with short cook times, such as cookies and biscuits.
4. Check foods for doneness at minimum time.
5. Use utensil size recommended in recipe.
6. Refer to charts on pages 74 through 77 for detailed information.

| FOOD | | Conventional Oven Temperature | Convection Oven Temperature | Comments |
|---|---|---|---|---|
| *Beef* | Tender Roasts | 325° | 325° | Roasts will cook in about ¼ less time. |
| | Pot Roast, Swiss Steak | 325° | 300° to 325° | |
| *Pork* | Roasts | 325° | 325° | Roasts will cook in about ¼ less time. |
| | Chops | 350° to 375° | 325° to 350° | |
| | Ham (fully cooked) | 325° | 325° | Roasts will cook in about ¼ less time. |
| *Lamb* | Roasts | 325° | 325° | Roasts will cook in about ⅓ less time. |
| *Poultry* | Whole Chicken | 375° | 350° | Reduce temperature and cook time. |
| | Chicken Pieces | 325° | 325° to 350° | Cook times are about the same as conventional. |
| | Turkey (unstuffed) | 325° | 325° | Turkey cooks in about ⅓ less time. |
| *Fish* | Steaks, Fillets (1 to 2 lbs.) | 400° to 450° | 325° to 375° | Cook times are about the same as conventional; temperature is reduced. |
| *Vegetables* | Acorn Squash | 350° | 325° | Cook times are about the same as conventional. |
| | Baked Potatoes | 425° | 400° | Reduce temperature and cook time. |
| *Main Dishes* | Casseroles | 350° | 325° to 350° | Casseroles will generally bake in 5 to 10 minutes less time. |
| | Meat Loaf (1 ½ lb.) | 350° | 325° | Cook time is about the same as conventional. |
| | Quiche | 350° | 325° | Cook time is about the same as conventional. |
| *Breads* | Yeast Bread | 375° | 325° | Use offset rack in bottom (A) shelf position. |
| | Quick Bread | 350° | 325° | Quick breads will cook in about the same or slightly less time. |
| | Corn Bread | 425° | 400° | |
| | Biscuits | 450° to 500° | 425° | Cook time is slightly longer. |
| *Desserts* | Layer Cakes | 350° | 300° | Use third (C) shelf position. |
| | Cookies | 350° to 375° | 325° | Use Multi-Shelf feature. |
| | Pies (2-crust) | 375° | 400° | |

# *Introduction*

## *Multi-Shelf Baking*

**Because heated air is circulated evenly throughout the oven, foods can be baked with excellent results on two or three shelves at a time.**

**Multi-Shelf baking may increase cook times slightly for some foods but the overall result is time saved.**

**For recommended shelf and pan placement in your oven model, refer to the Use and Care Guide.**

**Oven cavity configuration may vary from model to model. Refer to the Use and Care Guide for specific information concerning your model.**

When baking on 3 shelves, divide oven into thirds by placing the offset rack in the bottom (A) shelf position and straight racks in second (B) and fourth (D) shelf position.

For two-shelf baking, place the offset rack in the bottom (A) shelf position. Place the straight shelf in the third (C) shelf position.

When baking four cake layers, four pies or four loaves of bread, stagger pan placement on two shelves (as shown) for best browning.

Allow 4 to 5 inches between pans when baking loaves of yeast breads, quick breads or loaf cake for best circulation of heated air.

## *Roasting Techniques*

**Roasts cooked in a convection oven are richly browned with tender, juicy interiors. In most cases, cook times will be less in the convection oven.**

**To assure the desired degree of doneness, use the temperature probe provided with the oven and the convection roast setting. (See page 76 for internal temperatures.)**

**Roasting pans may vary from oven to oven. For your particular oven model, refer to the Use and Care Guide.**

The special roasting pan allows heated air to circulate over and under the roast. As a result, roasts are deliciously browned on all sides.

To insert probe, measure the distance to the center of the roast by laying the temperature probe on top of the meat. Mark with thumb and forefinger where the edge of the meat comes on the probe.

Insert the probe horizontally up to the point marked off with your finger. Make sure that tip of probe is in center of meat.

After removing probe from roast, leave probe attached to receptacle in oven wall until cool. Then remove probe and clean.

Because of variation in oven cavity design, location of the probe receptacle may differ from model to model. Refer to the Use and Care Guide for information concerning your particular model.

# Appetizers

▲ *Vegetable Crispers, Spicy Chicken Wings and Cocktail Reubens*

*Place buttered vegetables into plastic bag with crumb mixture and shake to coat evenly.*

## Vegetable Crispers

½ cup dry bread crumbs
½ cup grated Parmesan cheese
1 teaspoon tarragon leaves, crushed
1 teaspoon paprika
¼ teaspoon salt
Dash pepper
1 cup broccoli flowerets
1 cup cauliflower flowerets
1 medium zucchini, sliced ½ -inch thick
12 small whole mushrooms
½ cup butter, melted

Combine bread crumbs, Parmesan cheese, tarragon, paprika, salt and pepper in plastic bag. Taking several pieces at a time, dip broccoli, cauliflower, zucchini and mushrooms in melted butter. Place into plastic bag with crumb mixture and shake to coat evenly. Repeat until all vegetables are coated. Arrange in single layer in lightly greased 3-quart oblong glass baking dish. Convection Bake at 350°F. for 15 to 18 minutes or until lightly browned.

**Makes about 40 appetizers**

## Cocktail Reubens

36 slices cocktail rye bread, toasted
½ cup Thousand Island dressing
1 (8 oz.) can sauerkraut, rinsed and drained
¼ lb. thinly-sliced corned beef
1 (6 oz.) pkg. Swiss cheese slices, each slice cut into 4 squares

Arrange bread slices on baking sheet. Spread each slice with about ¾ teaspoon Thousand Island dressing. Add small amount of sauerkraut and corned beef to each slice. Top each with 1 square Swiss cheese. Convection Bake at 325°F. for 5 to 8 minutes or until cheese melts and edges are lightly browned.

**Makes 36 appetizers**

## Spicy Chicken Wings

½ cup sour cream
2 tablespoons red onion, finely chopped
1 clove garlic, crushed
¼ cup fresh parsley, minced
1 cup mayonnaise
¼ cup blue cheese, crumbled
1 tablespoon lemon juice
¼ teaspoon seasoned salt
¼ teaspoon freshly ground black pepper
⅛ teaspoon cayenne pepper
½ cup butter, melted
1 teaspoon hot sauce
¼ teaspoon salt
20 chicken wings, separated into 2 pieces

**For dip:** In small mixing bowl, combine sour cream, onion, garlic, parsley, mayonnaise, blue cheese, lemon juice, seasoned salt, pepper and cayenne pepper. Mix well and refrigerate.

In small mixing bowl, combine melted butter, hot sauce and salt. Place chicken wings in 10x15x1-inch jelly roll pan. Brush wings with butter mixture. Convection Bake at 375°F. for 20 to 25 minutes or until golden brown. Serve with dip above.

**Makes 8 to 10 appetizer servings**

## Artichoke Dip

1 (14 oz.) can artichoke hearts, drained and finely chopped
1 cup mayonnaise
1 cup grated Parmesan cheese
¼ teaspoon garlic salt
Paprika

In 8-inch square glass baking dish, mix chopped artichokes with mayonnaise, Parmesan cheese and garlic salt. Sprinkle with paprika. Convection Bake at 350°F. for 15 to 20 minutes or until heated through and top is light brown.

**Makes 2 cups**

# Appetizers

## Oriental Meatballs

1 lb. ground beef
1 lb. ground pork
½ cup canned water chestnuts, drained, finely chopped
¼ cup green pepper, finely chopped
3 green onions, chopped
¼ teaspoon salt
2 tablespoons soy sauce
2 tablespoons pineapple juice

**Sauce:**
1 (20 oz.) can chunk pineapple
½ cup water
2 tablespoons vinegar
1 tablespoon soy sauce
¼ cup brown sugar, packed
2 tablespoons cornstarch
1 tablespoon instant beef bouillon granules

In large mixing bowl, combine beef, pork, water chestnuts, green pepper, onions, salt, soy sauce and pineapple juice; mix well. Shape into 1-inch meatballs. Arrange meatballs in bottom of broil pan. Convection Bake at 350°F. for 25 to 30 minutes or until done; drain. Set aside and keep warm.

Drain pineapple, reserving liquid. In 4-cup glass measure, combine reserved pineapple juice, water, vinegar, soy sauce, brown sugar, cornstarch and bouillon. Stir until smooth. Microwave at HIGH (10) 4 to 5 minutes, until mixture thickens; stir after 2 minutes. Add pineapple. Pour sauce over meatballs.

**Makes 45 to 50 meatballs**

## Tiny Chicken Turnovers

½ (8 oz.) pkg. cream cheese, softened
½ cup butter, softened
1 cup all-purpose flour
1 cup cooked chicken, finely chopped
1 tablespoon onion, finely chopped
1 tablespoon sweet red pepper, finely chopped
2 tablespoons mayonnaise
1 teaspoon Dijon mustard
¼ teaspoon salt
⅛ teaspoon white pepper
1 egg, beaten

Beat cream cheese and butter together until light and fluffy. Blend in flour to make a soft dough. Turn out onto floured surface and knead lightly 10 to 12 strokes. Wrap in plastic wrap and refrigerate until firm enough to handle.

Combine chicken, onion, red pepper, mayonnaise, mustard, salt and pepper; blend thoroughly. Set aside while rolling out dough.

Roll dough on well-floured surface to 1/16-inch thickness. Cut into 3-inch rounds. Place one heaping teaspoon filling on each pastry round. Brush edges of pastry with egg. Fold pastry rounds in half over filling. Seal edges together with a fork. Brush tops with remaining egg. Convection Bake at 375°F. for 13 to 16 minutes or until golden.

**Makes about 20 appetizers**

▲ *Sausage Muffin Teasers and Tiny Chicken Turnovers*

## Sausage Muffin Teasers

½ lb. hot bulk pork
  sausage
2 cups all-purpose flour
1 tablespoon baking
  powder
1 tablespoon sugar
¼ teaspoon salt
⅛ teaspoon thyme
Dash cayenne pepper
1 cup milk
1 egg, slightly beaten
¼ cup vegetable oil
½ cup extra sharp
  Cheddar cheese,
  shredded
2 tablespoons onion,
  finely chopped

Brown sausage over medium heat, stirring to crumble. Drain well; set aside. In medium bowl, combine flour, baking powder, sugar, salt, thyme and cayenne pepper; make a well in center of mixture. Combine milk, egg and oil. Add to dry ingredients, stirring just until moistened. Stir in sausage, cheese and onion.

Spoon batter into greased 1¾ x1-inch muffin pans, filling three-fourths full. Convection Bake at 350°F. for 15 to 18 minutes. Remove from pans immediately.

**Makes 5 dozen muffins**

# Appetizers

## Sausage Crescents

*Spread sausage mixture down the center of dough.*

½ lb. lean bulk sausage
⅓ cup onion, chopped
1 tablespoon catsup
1 teaspoon fresh lemon juice
½ teaspoon Italian seasoning
¼ teaspoon garlic powder
1 (8 oz.) pkg. crescent roll dough
1 egg, beaten

Sauté sausage and onion over medium-high heat until meat is browned. Drain. Stir in catsup, lemon juice, Italian seasoning and garlic powder. Set aside to allow to cool. Cut pastry into 4 rectangles. Divide sausage mixture into fourths. Spread sausage mixture down center of dough. Brush long edges of pastry with beaten egg and fold over to seal, enclosing sausage completely. Brush dough with beaten egg. Cut each length into fourths. Arrange on well-greased baking sheet. Convection Bake at 350°F. for 9 to 12 minutes.

**Makes 16 appetizers**

## Barbecue Baby Back Ribs

*Cut each roll into 4 slices and arrange on baking sheet.*

2 lbs. baby back ribs, cut in serving size pieces
1 medium onion, chopped
2 cups hot tap water
Bottled Barbecue Sauce

Place ribs and onion in shallow baking dish; cover. Convection Bake at 350°F. for 40 minutes; drain. Pour barbecue sauce over ribs. Continue baking 25 to 30 minutes or until tender, basting frequently with sauce.

**Makes 6 servings**

## Hot Ham Spread

1 (8 oz.) pkg. cream cheese, softened
1 cup Swiss cheese, shredded
⅓ cup mayonnaise
2 tablespoons Dijon mustard
1 (6 ¾ oz.) can chunk ham, drained and flaked (or 1 cup finely chopped cooked ham)
2 tablespoons celery, minced
2 tablespoons onion, minced
2 tablespoons fresh parsley, chopped
½ teaspoon dillweed
¼ cup pecans, chopped

Combine all ingredients except pecans. Spread mixture into a 9-inch pie plate or quiche dish. Convection Bake at 325°F. for 15 minutes. Sprinkle with pecans. Serve with crackers.

**Makes about 2½ cups**

## Party Quiche Squares

½ cup onion,
  finely chopped
¼ cup sweet red pepper,
  finely chopped
2 tablespoons butter
1 (6 oz.) jar marinated
  artichoke hearts,
  chopped and drained
1 (16 oz.) can crabmeat,
  drained and flaked
4 eggs, beaten
2 cups sharp Cheddar
  cheese, shredded
¼ cup fine dry bread
  crumbs
2 tablespoons fresh
  parsley, minced
¼ teaspoon cayenne
  pepper
⅛ teaspoon thyme

Sauté onions and red pepper in butter until tender; cool slightly. Combine onion mixture, artichoke hearts, crabmeat, eggs, cheese, bread crumbs, parsley, cayenne pepper and thyme; mix well. Spoon into a lightly greased 11x7x2-inch baking dish. Convection Bake at 300°F. for 30 to 35 minutes or until set. Let stand 10 minutes. Cut into 1-inch squares.

**Makes 6 dozen**

## Brie In Pastry

1 sheet (half of a 17 ¼ oz.
  pkg.) puff pastry,
  thawed and unfolded
1 (14 to 18 oz.) round of
  Brie cheese
1 egg, beaten

Roll pastry to form a 12-inch square. Cut a 1-inch strip from each side of square. Roll 3 of the strips to 18-inch length and braid or twist to make 1 strip.

Place Brie, top down, in center of square of dough. Wrap dough over cheese, completely enclosing cheese. Moisten edges of dough with water and seal well. Place sealed-side down on baking sheet. Moisten bottom side of dough and gently press braid around side; press ends together to seal. Use remaining strip of dough to make decorative cutouts for top.

Using a pastry brush, brush egg over dough. Convection Bake at 350°F. for 15 to 20 minutes or until pastry is puffed and lightly browned. Let stand 20 minutes before serving.

**Makes 1 round**

*Wrap dough over cheese to completely enclose. Moisten edges with water to seal.*

## Sugar Glazed Walnuts

½ cup butter, melted
1 cup brown sugar, packed
1 teaspoon cinnamon
1 lb. walnut halves
  (about 4 cups)

In 1 ½-quart casserole, combine melted butter, brown sugar and cinnamon. Microwave at HIGH (10) 2 to 3 minutes; stir after 1 minute. Add nuts and mix to coat. Spread walnuts on baking sheet. Convection Bake at 325°F. for 10 to 12 minutes. Spread on wax paper to cool. Refrigerate in airtight container.

**Makes 1 pound**

*Gently press braid around side and press ends to seal.*

# *Meats*

▲ *Beef Rib Eye Roast with Mushroom Sauce*

## *Beef Rib Eye Roast with Mushroom Sauce*

**1 cup water**
**¼ cup bourbon**
**1 tablespoon lemon juice**
**1 tablespoon steak sauce**
**½ teaspoon garlic salt**
**½ teaspoon lemon pepper**
**¼ teaspoon cayenne pepper**
**1 (4 to 5 lb.) beef rib eye roast**
**½ lb. fresh mushrooms, sliced**
**½ cup water**
**2 teaspoons instant beef bouillon granules**
**2 teaspoons browning sauce**
**2 tablespoons cornstarch**
**¼ cup water**

Combine 1 cup water, bourbon, lemon juice, steak sauce, garlic salt, lemon pepper and cayenne pepper. Pierce roast with a fork in several places. Place meat in 2-quart oblong glass baking dish. Pour marinade over roast and cover. Marinate in refrigerator 8 hours, turning occasionally. Drain and reserve ½ cup marinade.

Place roast on trivet in broiler pan. Convection Roast at 325°F. to desired doneness (see chart, page 76). Let stand 10 minutes before carving.

**Mushroom Sauce:** In 1½-quart casserole, combine reserved marinade, mushrooms, ½ cup water, bouillon granules and browning sauce. Microwave at HIGH (10) 2 to 3 minutes. Combine cornstarch and ¼ cup water; stir into mushroom mixture. Microwave at HIGH (10) 2 to 3 minutes, until thickened, stirring every minute.

Makes 10 to 12 servings

## Flank Steak Florentine

1½ to 1¾ lb. beef flank
    steak
½ cup fresh mushrooms,
    chopped
1 medium onion, chopped
1 small carrot,
    finely chopped
1 clove garlic, minced
3 tablespoons butter
1 (10 oz.) pkg. frozen
    chopped spinach,
    thawed and well drained
2 teaspoons instant beef
    bouillon granules
¼ cup hot water
1 (10¾ oz.) can cream of
    chicken soup
2 tablespoons capers,
    drained
2 tablespoons dry
    vermouth, optional
½ teaspoon curry powder
¼ teaspoon coriander
¼ teaspoon white pepper

Pound flank steak with a wooden mallet to ⅛-inch thickness; score with a sharp knife. Sauté mushrooms, onion, carrot and garlic in butter until vegetables are tender. Add spinach and blend well. Spread spinach mixture over steak. Starting at long side, roll steak in jelly roll fashion. Tie with string or secure with toothpicks.

Place steak, seam side down, in 2-quart oblong glass baking dish. Dissolve bouillon granules in hot water. Add soup, capers, vermouth, curry powder, coriander and pepper. Pour over steak; cover. Convection Bake at 325°F. for 1¼ to 1½ hours or until tender.

**Makes 4 servings**

## Barbecued Beef Brisket

1 cup catsup
2 tablespoons
    Worcestershire sauce
1 tablespoon Dijon
    mustard
1 tablespoon red wine
    vinegar
1 tablespoon brown sugar
½ teaspoon salt
¼ teaspoon garlic salt
¼ teaspoon celery salt
⅛ teaspoon cayenne
    pepper
1 (3 to 4 lb.) beef brisket

In small bowl, combine catsup, Worcestershire sauce, mustard, vinegar, sugar, salt, garlic salt, celery salt and cayenne pepper. Pierce brisket on both sides with a fork. Place in 3-quart oblong glass baking dish. Pour half of sauce over brisket; cover. Convection Bake at 325°F. for 1 hour. Turn meat over and add remaining sauce. Cover and continue baking 30 to 45 minutes or until tender.

**Makes 6 to 8 servings**

# Meats

## Italian Sirloin Roast

1 (4 to 5 lb.) boneless
    sirloin tip roast
2 tablespoons vegetable oil
1 cup onion, chopped
1 clove garlic, crushed
1 (8 oz.) can tomato sauce
1 (4 oz.) can mushroom
    pieces, drained
1 tablespoon red wine
    vinegar
3 tablespoons fresh
    parsley, chopped
1 tablespoon brown sugar
¾ teaspoon salt
½ teaspoon oregano
½ teaspoon basil
¼ teaspoon red pepper
    flakes
Hot cooked spaghetti
¼ cup all-purpose flour
¼ cup water

In ovenproof Dutch oven, brown roast on all sides in hot oil. Pour off drippings. Thoroughly combine onion, garlic, tomato sauce, mushrooms, vinegar, parsley, sugar, salt, oregano, basil and red pepper flakes. Pour over meat. Cover. Convection Bake at 300°F. for 3 hours or until tender.

Remove roast from pan and slice into serving pieces. Arrange over spaghetti and keep warm. Combine flour and water; stir until smooth. Stir into hot liquid. Cook over medium heat until thickened, stirring constantly. Pour over meat and spaghetti.

**Makes 8 to 10 servings**

## Savory Swiss Steak

1½ lb. boneless round
    steak, pounded
    ¼-inch thick
1 (15 oz.) can whole
    tomatoes, chopped
1 (8 oz.) can tomato sauce
1 (1¾ oz.) pkg. dry onion-
    mushroom soup mix
2 tablespoons fresh
    parsley, snipped
1 teaspoon basil
¼ teaspoon oregano
¼ teaspoon garlic powder

Cut steak into serving size portions. In 3-quart casserole, combine steak, tomatoes, tomato sauce, soup mix, parsley, basil, oregano and garlic powder. Cover. Convection Bake at 325°F. for 55 to 60 minutes or until tender.

**Makes 4 to 6 servings**

## Stuffed Peppers

▲ *Stuffed Peppers*

6 medium yellow,
   green or red peppers
1½ lbs. ground chuck
1 cup cooked long grain
   rice
½ cup onion, chopped
½ cup celery, diced
1 (2 oz.) jar sliced
   pimento, drained
1 clove garlic, minced
1 teaspoon salt
¼ teaspoon pepper
1 (10 ¾ oz.) can condensed
   tomato soup
½ teaspoon basil
½ cup sharp Cheddar
   cheese, shredded

Cut off tops of peppers. Remove seeds and membrane. In large bowl, combine beef, rice, onion, celery, pimento, garlic, salt and pepper. Fill peppers with meat mixture. Arrange in 3-quart oblong glass baking dish. Combine soup and basil; pour over stuffed peppers. Convection Bake at 325°F. for 40 to 45 minutes or until done. Spoon sauce over peppers and sprinkle with cheese before serving.

**Makes 6 servings**

## Hamburgers Deluxe

2 lbs. ground chuck
1 tablespoon
Worcestershire sauce
1 teaspoon salt
¼ teaspoon garlic powder
¼ teaspoon pepper
¼ cup onion, chopped
¼ cup green pepper,
   chopped
¼ cup sharp Cheddar
   cheese, shredded
2 tablespoons catsup
1 tablespoon prepared
   mustard
6 slices bacon
Toasted hamburger buns

In mixing bowl, combine ground chuck, Worcestershire sauce, salt, garlic powder and pepper. Form meat mixture into 12 thin patties, about 4½ inches in diameter.

Combine onion, green pepper, cheese, catsup and mustard. Place approximately 2 tablespoons mixture in center of 6 meat patties. Top with remaining meat patties, sealing edges well. Wrap each pattie with bacon slice; fasten securely with toothpick.

Place patties on rack of broiler pan. Broil at Hi Broil setting, 3 inches from heat for 9 minutes. Turn patties over and continue broiling 7 to 8 minutes for well done patties. Serve on toasted buns.

**Makes 6 servings**

# *Meats*

*Spread cheese mixture over meat within ½-inch from sides.*

*Carefully roll up meat mixture from the short side to form roll.*

## *Cheese-Stuffed Meat Loaf*

1½ cups soft
    bread crumbs
1 egg, slightly beaten
1½ teaspoons seasoned
    salt
¼ teaspoon pepper
½ cup milk
¾ cup onion, chopped,
    divided
1½ lbs. ground chuck
2 tablespoons green
    pepper, chopped
2 tablespoons celery,
    chopped
1 (2 oz.) jar sliced
    pimento, drained
1 tablespoon lemon juice
1 egg, slightly beaten
1 cup Cheddar cheese,
    shredded
½ cup soft bread crumbs

In large mixing bowl, combine 1½ cups bread crumbs, 1 egg, seasoned salt, pepper, milk, ½ cup chopped onion and ground chuck.

In 1½-quart casserole, combine ¼ cup chopped onion, green pepper, celery, pimento and lemon juice. Microwave at HIGH (10) 2 to 3 minutes until crisp-tender. Add egg; blend well. Stir in cheese and ½ cup bread crumbs.

On strip of wax paper, shape meat mixture into 14x7-inch rectangle. Spread cheese mixture over meat. Lifting wax paper for support, roll meat mixture from short side in jelly roll fashion. Place seam-side down in 9x5-inch glass loaf dish.

**Spicy Tomato Topping:** In small bowl, combine ¾ cup catsup, ¼ cup brown sugar, ¾ teaspoon dry mustard, ¼ teaspoon allspice and ⅛ teaspoon cloves.

Convection Bake at 325°F. for 55 minutes. Add tomato topping and continue baking for 5 minutes. Let stand 5 minutes.

**Makes 6 servings**

## *Veal Parmigiana*

2 (8 oz.) cans tomato sauce
1 teaspoon sugar
½ teaspoon garlic salt
¼ teaspoon oregano
⅛ teaspoon pepper
2 eggs, beaten
1 teaspoon salt
¼ teaspoon pepper
1½ cups fine dry
    bread crumbs
6 boneless veal cutlets,
    ½-inch thick
¼ cup olive oil
1 cup mozzarella cheese,
    shredded
⅓ cup grated Parmesan
    cheese

Combine tomato sauce, sugar, garlic salt, oregano and pepper; mix well. Set aside. In shallow dish, combine eggs, salt and pepper. Dip veal cutlets in egg mixture and dredge in crumbs. Brown on both sides in hot oil. Place cutlets in 2-quart oblong glass baking dish. Pour tomato sauce over cutlets. Convection Bake at 325°F. for 20 to 25 minutes. Sprinkle with mozzarella cheese and Parmesan cheese. Continue baking 5 minutes or until cheese melts.

**Makes 6 servings**

## Veal Roll-Ups

6 boneless veal cutlets,
　½ -inch thick
6 thin slices Swiss cheese
6 thin slices boiled ham
2 eggs
¼ cup butter, melted
½ cup dry bread crumbs
¼ cup all-purpose flour
1 teaspoon salt
½ teaspoon paprika
¼ teaspoon onion powder
¼ teaspoon sage
¼ teaspoon pepper
3 tablespoons butter

Pound each cutlet with wooden mallet to ¼ -inch thickness. Place 1 slice cheese and 1 slice ham on each piece of veal. Roll up firmly and fasten with a toothpick.

In small bowl, beat together eggs and ¼ cup butter. In shallow dish, combine bread crumbs, flour, salt, paprika, onion powder, sage and pepper. Dip veal rolls in egg mixture, then roll in crumb mixture. In large skillet, brown rolls in 3 tablespoons butter for 5 minutes. Place rolls in 2-quart oblong glass baking dish. Convection Bake at 350°F. for 35 to 40 minutes or until done.

**Makes 4 to 6 servings**

*Place cheese and ham on top of flattened veal cutlet.*

## Barbecued Spareribs

2 ½ to 3 lbs. pork
　spareribs, cut into
　2-rib pieces
1 medium onion, chopped
1 medium sweet red
　pepper, chopped
2 cloves garlic, minced
½ cup catsup
½ cup brown sugar,
　firmly packed
¼ cup molasses
2 tablespoons lemon juice
1 teaspoon prepared
　brown mustard
Dash hot sauce

Place ribs in 3-quart casserole; cover. Convection Bake at 350°F. for 40 minutes; drain. In small mixing bowl, combine onion, red pepper, garlic, catsup, sugar, molasses, lemon juice, mustard and hot sauce. Pour sauce over ribs. Cover and continue baking for 25 to 30 minutes.

**Makes 4 servings**

*Dip veal roll in egg mixture then roll in crumb mixture.*

## Sherried Peach Pork Chops

1 (16 oz.) can peach halves
¼ cup dry sherry
½ teaspoon coriander
¼ teaspoon cumin
¼ teaspoon ginger
⅛ teaspoon cayenne
　pepper
⅛ teaspoon garlic powder
4 loin pork chops,
　1-inch thick
⅓ cup chutney, coarsely
　chopped

Drain peaches, reserving syrup. Set peach halves aside. Combine reserved syrup, sherry, coriander, cumin, ginger, cayenne pepper and garlic powder; blend well. Place pork chops in shallow dish; pour marinade over chops. Let stand 1 hour in refrigerator, turning over once. Remove chops from marinade. Discard marinade. Place chops on lightly greased rack of broiling pan. Broil on Hi Broil setting 6 inches from heat for 15 minutes. Turn chops over and continue broiling 12 minutes. Fill peach halves with chutney. Arrange filled peach halves around chops. Continue broiling 3 minutes.

**Makes 4 servings**

# Meats

▲ *Apple-Stuffed Pork Chops*

*To form a pocket, use a sharp knife to cut pork chop through center.*

## Apple-Stuffed Pork Chops

1 ½ **cups herb-seasoned**
    **stuffing mix**
1 **cup apple, diced**
¼ **cup onion,**
    **finely chopped**
3 **tablespoons raisins**
½ **cup orange juice**
2 **tablespoons butter,**
    **melted**
1 **tablespoon grated**
    **orange rind**
½ **teaspoon salt**
¼ **teaspoon cinnamon**
¼ **teaspoon allspice**
⅛ **teaspoon pepper**
4 **center-cut pork chops,**
    **1-inch thick**
½ **cup currant jelly**
2 **tablespoons orange juice**

In mixing bowl, combine stuffing mix, apple, onion, raisins, ½ cup orange juice, butter, orange rind, salt, cinnamon, allspice and pepper. Cut a pocket in each pork chop. Divide stuffing evenly among chops.

Arrange chops in 2-quart oblong glass baking dish. In 1-cup glass measure, combine currant jelly and 2 tablespoons orange juice. Microwave at HIGH (10) 1 to 2 minutes; stir well. Brush half of mixture over chops. Convection Bake at 350°F. for 45 to 50 minutes or until tender. Spoon remaining jelly mixture over chops before serving.

**Makes 4 servings**

## Glazed Pork Roast with Pineapple Salsa

1 large pineapple, peeled,
  cored, finely chopped
1 small sweet red pepper,
  finely chopped
1 small green pepper,
  finely chopped
1 small red onion,
  finely chopped
3 tablespoons fresh
  parsley, snipped
2 tablespoons fresh chives,
  snipped
2 tablespoons lemon juice
1 tablespoon vegetable oil
¼ teaspoon salt
¼ teaspoon cayenne
  pepper
⅛ teaspoon white pepper
1 (4 to 5 lb.) pork loin roast

Combine pineapple, green and red pepper, onion, parsley, chives, lemon juice, oil, salt, cayenne pepper and white pepper. Cover and refrigerate 2 hours.

Place roast on trivet in broiler pan. Convection Roast at 325°F. until well done (see chart, page 76). During last 10 minutes of cooking time, baste roast occasionally with Pineapple Glaze (see below). Let stand 10 minutes before carving. Serve with salsa.

**Pineapple Glaze:** Combine ½ cup pineapple preserves, 1 tablespoon orange juice, ¼ teaspoon cinnamon and ⅛ teaspoon ginger.

Makes 6 to 8 servings

## Lemon Pork Chops

4 center-cut pork chops,
  ¾ -inch thick
½ teaspoon salt
¼ teaspoon pepper
⅛ teaspoon thyme
4 onion slices
4 lemon slices
½ cup chili sauce
1 tablespoon brown sugar

Sprinkle chops with salt, pepper and thyme. Arrange chops in 3-quart casserole. Combine chili sauce and brown sugar; pour over chops. Place onion and lemon slice on each chop. Cover. Convection Bake at 325°F. for 35 to 40 minutes or until done.

Makes 4 servings

## Peachy Glazed Ham Slice

1 (8¾ oz.) can peach
  slices, drained
2 tablespoons honey
2 tablespoons lemon juice
¼ teaspoon ground
  allspice
1 teaspoon grated
  lemon rind
1 (1¼ -inch thick) fully
  cooked boneless
  ham slice

In a blender container, combine peach slices, honey, lemon juice and allspice. Cover and blend until smooth; stir in lemon rind. Set aside.

Slash edges of ham at 1-inch intervals. Place ham on rack of broil pan. Broil at Hi Broil setting 2 inches from heat for 7 minutes. Turn and brush with peach mixture. Continue broiling 6 to 7 minutes, brushing frequently with sauce.

Makes 6 to 8 servings

# Meats

## Classic Ham Loaf

1 lb. ground cooked ham
½ lb. ground fresh pork
½ cup soft bread crumbs
½ cup water
1 egg
½ cup onion,
   finely chopped
¼ teaspoon marjoram
¼ teaspoon pepper

Combine all ingredients. Place in 9x5-inch glass loaf dish. Convection Bake at 325°F. for 45 to 50 minutes or until done. Let stand 5 minutes.

**Makes 6 servings**

## Savory Stuffed Lamb Chops

¼ cup onion, chopped
¼ cup celery, chopped
1 clove garlic, minced
3 tablespoons butter
1 cup cooked rice
1 (2 oz.) can mushroom
   pieces, drained
1 tablespoon fresh parsley,
   chopped
½ teaspoon salt
½ teaspoon thyme
¼ teaspoon rosemary
6 shoulder lamb chops,
   1½-inch thick with
   pocket

Saute onion, celery and garlic in butter until crisp-tender. Combine vegetable mixture, rice, mushrooms, parsley, salt, thyme and rosemary. Fill pockets in lamb chops with rice mixture, dividing mixture evenly among chops. Place chops in baking pan. Convection Bake at 300°F. for 45 to 50 minutes or until tender.

**Makes 6 servings**

## Leg of Lamb with Mustard Glaze

½ cup Dijon mustard
1 teaspoon basil
¼ teaspoon thyme
¼ teaspoon white pepper
2 tablespoons vegetable oil
2 tablespoons
   Worcestershire sauce
1 (4 to 5 lb.) leg of lamb

Combine mustard, basil, thyme, pepper, oil and Worcestershire sauce. Pierce lamb in several places with fork. Place fat side up in shallow baking dish. Spread mustard mixture over lamb. Chill 2 hours.

Place roast on trivet in broiler pan. Convection Roast at 325°F. to desired doneness (see chart, page 76). Let stand 10 minutes before carving.

**Makes 6 to 8 servings**

▲ *Zesty Lamb Kabobs*

## Zesty Lamb Kabobs

1⅓ cups dry red wine
2 tablespoons vegetable oil
1 cup onion,
    finely chopped
2 cloves garlic, crushed
2 tablespoons Dijon
    mustard
1 bay leaf
¾ teaspoon salt
½ teaspoon pepper
½ teaspoon thyme
¼ teaspoon ginger
2 lbs. lamb, cut in 1-inch
    cubes
2 large green peppers,
    cut in 1-inch squares
2 large red peppers,
    cut in 1-inch squares
3 medium onions,
    cut in eighths
3 tablespoons cornstarch
Cooked rice

In 2-quart casserole or self-sealing plastic bag, combine wine, oil, onion, garlic, mustard, bay leaf, salt, pepper, thyme and ginger. Add lamb cubes. Cover and marinate in refrigerator several hours or overnight. Remove lamb from marinade. Reserve marinade.

On 8-inch skewers, thread red or green pepper square, onion chunk and lamb cube. Repeat, ending with onion chunk and pepper square. Place kabobs on rack of broil pan. Broil at High Broil setting 3 inches from heat for 6 to 8 minutes for medium doneness. Brush with marinade and turn skewers often. Place kabobs on a bed of cooked rice; keep warm.

In 4-cup glass measure, combine reserved marinade and cornstarch; stir until smooth. Microwave at HIGH (10) 4 to 5 minutes, until thickened, stirring every 2 minutes. Remove bay leaf. Serve sauce with kabobs.

**Makes 4 servings**

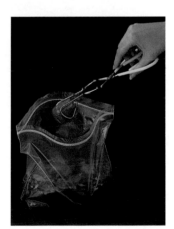

*Self-sealing bags may be used for marinating meats and vegetables.*

# Poultry

▲ *Mint-Laced Chicken*

*Place fresh mint leaves in cavity of chicken.*

## Mint-Laced Chicken

1 (2 ½ to 3 lb.)
   whole chicken
½ teaspoon salt
¼ teaspoon garlic powder
¼ teaspoon lemon pepper
1 cup fresh mint leaves
½ cup butter, melted
2 tablespoons lemon juice

Rinse chicken with cold water and pat dry. Combine salt, garlic powder and lemon pepper. Sprinkle inside chicken cavity. Place mint leaves in cavity of chicken.

Combine butter and lemon juice; brush over outside of chicken. Place chicken on trivet in broiler pan. Convection Bake at 350°F. for 1 to 1 ¼ hours.

### Makes 4 to 6 servings

## Sweet and Tangy Chicken

1 (2 ½ to 3 ½ lb.) chicken,
   cut up
¼ cup mayonnaise
1 (1 ¾ oz.) pkg. dry onion
   soup mix
1 cup bottled Russian
   dressing
½ cup apricot preserves
½ cup pineapple preserves

Arrange chicken in 2-quart oblong glass baking dish. In small mixing bowl, combine mayonnaise, onion soup mix, dressing and preserves. Pour over chicken. Convection Bake at 350°F. for 40 to 45 minutes.

### Makes 4 servings

## Chicken A La Roma

¾ cup green onion,
   thinly sliced
2 cloves garlic, minced
½ lb. fresh mushrooms,
   sliced
2 tablespoons olive oil
1 (8 oz.) can tomato sauce
1 (6 oz.) can tomato paste
½ cup dry white wine
½ cup ripe olives, sliced
1 tablespoon instant
   chicken bouillon
   granules
2 teaspoons parsley flakes
1 teaspoon basil
1 teaspoon oregano
1 teaspoon salt
¼ teaspoon pepper
1 (2 ½ to 3 lb.) chicken,
   cut up
1 (6 oz.) jar marinated
   artichoke hearts,
   drained
¼ cup grated Parmesan
   cheese

Sauté onion, garlic and mushrooms in oil until tender.

Combine tomato sauce, tomato paste, white wine, olives, bouillon, parsley, basil, oregano, salt and pepper. Add onion mixture; blend well.

Place chicken pieces in baking dish. Add tomato mixture. Convection Bake at 325°F. for 40 minutes. Arrange artichoke hearts around chicken and top with Parmesan cheese. Continue baking for 10 to 15 minutes or until done.

Makes 4 to 6 servings

## Chicken Italiano

½ lb. fresh mushrooms,
   sliced
½ cup onion, chopped
2 cloves garlic, minced
2 tablespoons olive oil
6 boneless chicken breast
   halves, skinned
1 cup spaghetti sauce
⅔ cup dry white wine
¾ teaspoon Italian
   seasoning
¼ teaspoon basil
¼ cup grated Parmesan
   cheese
¼ teaspoon red pepper
   flakes

In large skillet, sauté mushrooms, onion and garlic in oil until tender. Add chicken; sauté until lightly browned on both sides. Transfer chicken and vegetables to 3-quart casserole. Combine spaghetti sauce, wine, Italian seasoning and basil; pour over chicken. Sprinkle with Parmesan cheese and red pepper flakes. Convection Bake at 325°F. for 25 to 30 minutes.

Makes 4 to 6 servings

*To bone chicken breast, split the breast in half lengthwise.*

*Starting at the breast bone side of the chicken, slice meat away from the bone.*

# Poultry

## Crescent-Wrapped Curried Chicken Breasts

2 cups water
6 boneless chicken breast
   halves, skinned
1 tablespoon curry powder
1 (10 oz.) pkg. frozen
   chopped spinach,
   thawed and drained
1 (8 oz.) container
   sour cream
1 (3 oz.) pkg. cream cheese
1 teaspoon coriander
3 (8 oz.) pkgs.
   crescent rolls
1 cup Swiss cheese,
   shredded, divided

**Butter Sauce:**
½ cup butter
1 tablespoon lemon juice
¼ teaspoon pepper
¼ teaspoon dry mustard
3 egg yolks, beaten

In 3-quart casserole, place water, chicken and curry. Microwave at MEDIUM HIGH (7) 8 to 10 minutes; stir after 5 minutes. Drain and set aside. In medium mixing bowl, combine spinach, sour cream, cream cheese and coriander. Divide each package of crescent rolls in half. Press perforations together to seal. On each square place ¼ cup Swiss cheese, one chicken breast and about ⅓ cup spinach mixture. Fold dough in half over chicken to form triangles; press edges to seal. Place on ungreased baking sheet. Convection Bake at 325°F. for 20 to 25 minutes or until golden brown. Transfer to serving platter and keep warm.

**Makes 4 servings**

In 2-cup glass measure, place butter, lemon juice, pepper and mustard. Microwave at HIGH (10) 1 minute until butter melts. With a wire whisk, blend in egg yolks. Microwave at MEDIUM (5) 30 seconds to 1 minute. Pour over chicken.

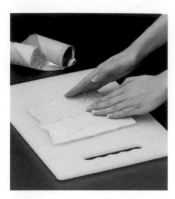

*Press crescent roll perforations together to seal.*

*Top with chicken and ⅓ cup spinach mixture.*

*Fold dough over chicken to form a triangle and seal edges.*

## Citrus Chicken

⅓ cup orange juice
⅓ cup lemon juice
⅓ cup lime juice
1 tablespoon grated
   orange zest
1 clove garlic, minced
1 teaspoon sugar
Dash hot sauce
2 tablespoons vegetable oil
4 chicken leg quarters

In small saucepan, combine orange juice, lemon juice, lime juice, orange zest, garlic, sugar and hot sauce. Cook over medium heat until sugar is dissolved, stirring occasionally. Remove from heat and whisk in oil; cool.

Place chicken in shallow dish and prick skin in several places with a fork. Pour marinade over chicken. Cover and refrigerate 2 hours, turning occasionally. Remove chicken from marinade and place chicken skin side down on lightly greased rack of broil pan. Discard marinade. Broil at Lo Broil setting 8 inches from heat for 16 minutes. Turn chicken over and continue broiling 12 to 14 minutes or until done.

**Makes 4 to 8 servings**

▲ *Chicken with Spicy Cheddar Sauce*

## Chicken with Spicy Cheddar Sauce

½ **cup cornflake crumbs**
½ **teaspoon paprika**
¼ **teaspoon garlic powder**
4 **boneless chicken breast
  halves, skinned**
½ **cup cheese spread with
  jalapeno peppers**
¼ **cup pitted ripe olives,
  sliced**
1 **(2 oz.) jar sliced pimento,
  drained and chopped**

In medium mixing bowl, combine cornflake crumbs, paprika and garlic powder. Rinse chicken in water, then coat with crumb mixture. Place chicken in 2-quart oblong glass baking dish. Convection Bake at 350°F. for 40 to 45 minutes or until done. Transfer chicken to serving platter and keep warm.

In 2-cup glass measure, combine cheese spread, olives and pimento. Microwave at HIGH (10) 1 minute until heated through. Pour sauce over chicken.

Makes 4 servings

## Chicken Parmesan

¾ **cup seasoned dry
  bread crumbs**
¼ **cup grated Parmesan
  cheese**
¼ **teaspoon paprika**
1 **egg, beaten**
¼ **cup water**
2 **(1 to 1 ¼ lb.) boneless
  chicken breasts, skinned,
  split and pounded thin**
1 **cup spaghetti sauce**
1 **cup mozzarella cheese,
  shredded**

In small mixing bowl, combine bread crumbs, Parmesan cheese and paprika. Set aside. In shallow dish, blend egg and water. Dip chicken breasts in egg mixture and then in bread crumb mixture. In 2-quart oblong glass baking dish, arrange chicken. Pour spaghetti sauce over top and sprinkle with mozzarella cheese. Convection Bake at 375°F. for 30 to 35 minutes.

Makes 4 servings

*Pound chicken breast to ¼-inch thickness.*

# Poultry

▲ *Chicken and Peppers in White Wine Sauce*

## Chicken & Peppers in White Wine Sauce

½ lb. bacon, cut into
   ¾ -inch pieces
1 (3 lb.) chicken, cut up
1 cup onion, coarsely
   chopped
⅔ cup green pepper,
   coarsely chopped
⅔ cup red pepper,
   coarsely chopped
½ cup black olives, sliced
1 teaspoon sage
¼ teaspoon thyme
¼ teaspoon salt
¼ teaspoon pepper
1 cup dry white wine

In large skillet, cook bacon until crisp. Drain, reserving 3 tablespoons drippings. Brown chicken on both sides in reserved drippings. Transfer chicken to 3-quart oblong glass baking dish. Add onion, green pepper, red pepper, olives, sage, thyme, salt and pepper. Pour wine over chicken and vegetables. Cover. Convection Bake at 350°F. for 40 to 45 minutes or until done.

**Makes 6 servings**

## Oven Barbecued Chicken

1 (3 lb.) chicken, cut up
1 large onion, sliced
½ cup celery, sliced
¼ cup water
½ teaspoon salt
⅛ teaspoon pepper
¾ cup catsup
¼ cup honey
1 tablespoon
   Worcestershire sauce
1 tablespoon prepared
   mustard
1 tablespoon cider vinegar
⅛ teaspoon allspice

Place chicken pieces, skin side up, in large baking pan. Arrange onion slices and celery around chicken pieces. Pour water over chicken. Sprinkle with salt and pepper. Convection Bake at 300°F. for 25 minutes. In small bowl, combine catsup, honey, Worcestershire sauce, mustard, vinegar and allspice. Pour sauce over chicken; bake 20 to 25 minutes longer or until done.

**Makes 4 to 6 servings**

## Baked Chicken Bites

1½ cups bread crumbs
½ cup grated Parmesan
   cheese
1 tablespoon thyme
1 tablespoon basil
1 teaspoon salt
½ teaspoon lemon pepper
¾ cup butter, melted
½ teaspoon hot sauce
6 whole boneless chicken
   breasts, cubed

In shallow dish, combine bread crumbs, Parmesan cheese, thyme, basil, salt and lemon pepper. Mix well. In small mixing bowl, combine butter and hot sauce. Dip chicken pieces in butter and coat with bread crumb mixture. Place coated chicken pieces in 15x10x1-inch jelly roll pan. Convection Bake at 375°F. for 20 to 25 minutes or until chicken is golden brown.

**Makes 8 to 10 servings**

*Place coated chicken pieces in jelly roll pan.*

## Hot Chicken Salad

1½ cups cooked chicken,
   diced
½ cup celery,
   finely chopped
½ cup slivered almonds,
   toasted
½ cup butter cracker
   crumbs
¼ cup onion, chopped
1 (10¾ oz.) can cream of
   chicken soup
½ cup mayonnaise
½ teaspoon salt
¾ cup Cheddar cheese,
   shredded

In 1½-quart casserole, combine chicken, celery, almonds, cracker crumbs, onion, chicken soup, mayonnaise and salt. Mix well. Convection Bake at 325°F. for 30 minutes. Sprinkle with cheese and continue baking 5 minutes or until cheese melts.

**Makes 4 servings**

# Poultry

▲ *Teriyaki Cornish Hens*

### Teriyaki Cornish Hens

1 ½ **tablespoons cornstarch**
3 **tablespoons brown sugar**
¼ **teaspoon dry mustard**
⅛ **teaspoon ginger**
½ **cup teriyaki sauce**
¼ **cup orange juice**
4 **(1 to 1 ½ lb.) Cornish hens**
1 **(6 oz.) pkg. long grain**
  **and wild rice mix,**
  **cooked**
½ **cup dried apricots,**
  **finely chopped**

In 1-quart casserole, combine cornstarch, brown sugar, dry mustard and ginger. Add teriyaki sauce and orange juice; stir until smooth. Microwave at HIGH (10) 3 to 4 minutes, until thickened, stirring every minute. Set aside.

Remove giblets from hens and save for another use, if desired. Rinse hens with cold water and pat dry. In small mixing bowl, combine rice and apricots. Stuff hens with rice mixture and close cavities. Secure with toothpicks. Place hens, breast side up, on trivet in broiler pan. Convection Bake at 350°F. for 55 to 60 minutes. Brush frequently with reserved marinade during last 15 minutes of baking time.

Makes 4 servings

## Roast Duck with Orange Sauce

(4 to 5 lb.) duck
¼ cup butter, melted
? tablespoons cider
  vinegar
? tablespoons sugar
  cup chicken broth
½ cup orange juice
  tablespoon orange peel,
  grated
  teaspoon lemon juice
? tablespoons cornstarch

Tuck wing tips under back of duck. Brush with melted butter. Place breast side up on trivet in broiler pan. Set aside.

In 1½-quart casserole, combine vinegar and sugar. Microwave at HIGH (10) 2 minutes, until lightly browned; stir after 1 minute. Add broth, orange juice, orange peel, lemon juice and cornstarch; stir until smooth. Microwave at HIGH (10) 4 to 6 minutes, until clear and thickened, stirring every 2 minutes. Baste duck with orange sauce. Convection Bake at 325°F. for 1¾ to 2 hours, spooning off fat occasionally. Baste with reserved orange sauce frequently during last 15 minutes of baking time.

**Makes 6 servings**

## Mexican Turkey Loaf

2 lbs. ground turkey
2 cups soft bread crumbs
1 egg, beaten
2 cloves garlic, minced
½ cup onion, chopped
1 (8 oz.) can tomato sauce
2 tablespoons green
  chilies, chopped
½ teaspoon cumin
½ teaspoon chili powder
½ teaspoon salt
¼ teaspoon oregano
½ cup Cheddar cheese,
  shredded

In large mixing bowl, combine all ingredients except cheese. Spoon mixture into a 9x5-inch loaf pan, pressing firmly. Convection Bake at 325°F. for 1¼ hours. Sprinkle with cheese and bake 5 minutes longer.

**Makes 6 servings**

## Savory Turkey Squares with Cranberry Sauce

3 cups cooked turkey,
  chopped
2 cups bread cubes
½ cup celery, minced
¼ cup onion, minced
1 (2 oz.) jar diced
  pimento, drained
3 eggs, slightly beaten
⅔ cup milk
½ cup chicken broth
1 tablespoon lemon juice
½ teaspoon poultry
  seasoning
¼ teaspoon pepper

In large mixing bowl, combine turkey, bread cubes, celery, onion, pimento, eggs, milk, chicken broth, lemon juice, poultry seasoning and pepper. Mix well. Spoon mixture into a 2-quart oblong glass baking dish. Convection Bake at 325°F. for 35 to 40 minutes or until done. Let stand 10 minutes. Cut into squares. Serve with Cranberry Sauce.

**Makes 6 servings**

**Cranberry Sauce:** In small saucepan, combine 1 cup whole berry cranberry sauce, 3 tablespoons orange marmalade, 1 teaspoon prepared mustard, ½ teaspoon allspice and ¼ teaspoon ginger. Cook over medium heat until heated through. Makes about 1 cup.

# Fish & Seafood

▲ *Company Lobster Tails*

## Company Lobster Tails

¼ **cup seasoned dry
  bread crumbs**
2 **tablespoons fresh parsley,
  minced**
¼ **teaspoon onion powder**
⅛ **teaspoon paprika**
⅛ **teaspoon salt**
4 **(8 oz.) lobster tails,
  thawed**
¼ **cup butter, melted**
2 **tablespoons lemon juice**

In small bowl, combine bread crumbs, parsley, onion powder, paprika and salt; set aside.

With kitchen shears, cut lobster through center of soft under shell to the tail. Lift lobster out of shell by loosening with fingers, leaving meat attached to tail section. (Lobster meat will rest on shell.) Place lobster tails on rack of broil pan. Shield ends of tails with aluminum foil. Combine ¼ cup butter and 2 tablespoons lemon juice; brush over lobster tails. Broil at Lo Broil setting, 3 inches from heat for 9 minutes. Brush with remaining butter mixture. Broil 8 to 9 minutes longer or until done. Sprinkle evenly with crumb mixture. Serve with Lemon Butter.

**Lemon Butter:**  In small bowl, Microwave ½ cup butter and 2 tablespoons lemon juice at Medium (5) 1 to 2 minutes or until butter is melted.

**Makes 4 servings**

## Spiced Fish Bake

6 (4 oz.) fish fillets
1 teaspoon paprika
½ teaspoon salt
½ teaspoon lemon pepper
¼ teaspoon dry mustard
¼ teaspoon garlic powder
⅛ teaspoon poultry
   seasoning
Dash cayenne pepper
3 tablespoons butter,
   melted

Place fish on lightly greased baking sheet. Combine paprika, salt, lemon pepper, mustard, garlic powder, poultry seasoning and cayenne pepper. Sprinkle evenly over fish. Drizzle with melted butter. Convection Bake at 325°F. for 10 to 15 minutes or until fish flakes easily.

**Makes 6 servings**

## Baked Grouper with Creole Sauce

1 (8 oz.) can tomato sauce
1 tablespoon dry
   white wine
2 teaspoons sugar
1 teaspoon basil
½ teaspoon sage
½ teaspoon curry
½ teaspoon salt
¼ teaspoon oregano
¼ teaspoon red pepper
   flakes
4 (6 oz.) grouper fillets
¼ cup green onions, sliced

Combine tomato sauce, wine, sugar, basil, sage, curry, salt, oregano and pepper; blend well. Place fillets in lightly greased 2-quart oblong glass baking dish. Pour sauce over fish. Sprinkle with onions. Convection Bake at 350°F. for 20 to 25 minutes or until fish flakes easily.

**Makes 4 servings**

## Baked Sole Florentine

¼ cup onion, chopped
1 clove garlic, minced
2 teaspoons olive oil
1 (10 oz.) pkg. frozen
   chopped spinach,
   thawed and well drained
1 (2 oz.) jar diced pimento,
   drained
½ cup crumbled
   Feta cheese
1 teaspoon grated
   lemon rind
½ teaspoon salt
¼ teaspoon oregano
⅛ teaspoon white pepper
6 sole fillets (about
   1½ pounds)
Paprika

Sauté onion and garlic in olive oil until tender. Combine vegetable mixture, spinach, pimento, cheese, lemon rind, salt, oregano and pepper. Spread spinach mixture in lightly greased 2-quart oblong glass baking dish. Arrange fish over spinach; sprinkle with paprika. Convection Bake at 375°F. for 9 to 11 minutes or until fish flakes easily.

**Makes 6 servings**

# Fish & Seafood

▲ *Salmon Steaks*

*Sprinkle lemon pepper onto buttered dish for extra flavor.*

## Salmon Steaks

1 tablespoon butter
2 teaspoons lemon pepper
6 (5 oz.) salmon steaks
2 teaspoons lemon juice
1 teaspoon lemon pepper
½ teaspoon garlic powder
½ teaspoon onion powder
6 thin onion slices
3 lemon slices, halved
1 teaspoon dried tarragon
1 teaspoon paprika
Dash salt

Place butter in 3-quart oblong glass baking dish. Microwave at HIGH (10) 30 seconds until melted. Coat bottom of dish with butter and sprinkle with 2 teaspoons lemon pepper. Place salmon steaks in prepared dish. Sprinkle with lemon juice, 1 teaspoon lemon pepper, garlic powder and onion powder. Place one onion slice and one lemon slice on each salmon steak. Sprinkle with tarragon, paprika and salt. Convection Bake at 325°F. for 20 to 25 minutes or until fish flakes easily.

**Makes 6 servings**

## Baked Fish with Cheese

1 lb. haddock
1 tablespoon tarragon
½ teaspoon seasoned salt
2 tablespoons butter
¼ cup sour cream or
   yogurt
1 cup mozzarella cheese,
   shredded
Paprika

Arrange fish in 2-quart oblong glass baking dish. Sprinkle with tarragon and seasoned salt. Dot with butter. In small mixing bowl, blend sour cream or yogurt and mozzarella cheese. Set aside.

Convection Bake at 350°F. for 10 minutes. Top with sour cream mixture and continue baking 5 to 10 minutes longer. Sprinkle with paprika.

**Makes 3 to 4 servings**

## Baked Scrod

1 cup onion, thinly sliced
2 cups fresh mushrooms, thinly sliced
1 teaspoon thyme
¾ teaspoon oregano
¼ teaspoon salt
¼ teaspoon garlic powder
¼ teaspoon lemon pepper
2 tablespoons olive oil
Vegetable cooking spray
2 lbs. scrod, cut into 4 equal portions
2 teaspoons fresh parsley, snipped

Sauté onion, mushrooms, thyme, oregano, salt, garlic powder and lemon pepper in olive oil until onion is transparent and mushrooms are tender.

Cut aluminum foil into 4 (18 x 12-inch) pieces. Spray aluminum foil with cooking spray and place fish portions on foil. Spoon ¼ of filling over each portion of fish. Sprinkle with parsley. Fold foil, crimping edges to seal. Place foil wrapped fish on baking sheet. Convection Bake at 450°F. for 15 to 20 minutes.

**Makes 4 servings**

*Place fish on foil and spoon ¼ of vegetable filling over each portion.*

## Fish Almondine

½ cup slivered almonds
½ cup butter
1 lb. fish fillets
1 teaspoon lemon juice
1 teaspoon fresh parsley, snipped
¼ teaspoon salt
¼ teaspoon dillweed
⅛ teaspoon pepper

Sauté almonds in butter until almonds are golden brown. Remove almonds and set aside; reserve butter. Place fish in baking dish; coat both sides with reserved butter. Sprinkle with lemon juice, parsley, salt, dillweed, pepper and almonds. Convection Bake at 350°F. for 12 to 15 minutes.

**Makes 3 servings**

*Completely enclose fish in foil, and crimp edges to seal.*

## Salmon Loaf

2 (16 oz.) cans red salmon, drained with bone and skin removed
¾ cup dry bread crumbs
2 tablespoons grated Parmesan cheese
½ cup milk
1 egg, beaten
¼ cup butter, melted
½ teaspoon salt

In large mixing bowl, combine salmon, bread crumbs, Parmesan cheese, milk, egg, butter and salt. Mix well. Pack mixture firmly into 8x4x3-inch glass loaf dish. Convection Bake at 325°F. for 35 to 40 minutes.

**Makes 4 to 6 servings**

# Fish & Seafood

▲ *Swordfish with Orange Sauce*

## Swordfish with Orange Sauce

⅔ cup orange marmalade
⅓ cup pineapple juice
2 teaspoons prepared
  horseradish
¼ teaspoon garlic powder
¼ teaspoon coriander
Dash hot sauce
4 (6 oz.) swordfish steaks
3 tablespoons lime juice
2 tablespoons butter,
  melted

**For Orange Sauce:** In small saucepan, combine orange marmalade, pineapple juice, horseradish, garlic powder, coriander and hot sauce. Cook over medium-low heat 5 minutes. Set aside and keep warm.

Place swordfish steaks on lightly greased rack of broil pan. Combine lime juice and butter; brush over steaks. Broil at Lo Broil setting 4 inches from heat for 8 minutes. Turn fish over and continue broiling 8 to 10 minutes or until done. Brush occasionally with lime-butter mixture. Serve with Orange Sauce.

**Makes 4 servings**

## Scalloped Oysters

½ cup onion, chopped
½ cup green pepper,
  chopped
2 tablespoons butter
¼ cup butter, melted
2 cups buttery cracker
  crumbs
½ teaspoon salt
⅛ teaspoon pepper
2 (8 oz.) cans fresh oysters,
  drained
1 teaspoon
  Worcestershire sauce
1 cup evaporated milk

Saute onion and green pepper in 2 tablespoons butter until tender. Set aside. In small mixing bowl, combine ¼ cup butter, cracker crumbs, salt and pepper. Mix well.

In 2-quart casserole, place ⅓ crumb mixture, one can of oysters and half of onion and green pepper mixture. Repeat layers ending with cracker crumbs.

In small mixing bowl, combine Worcestershire sauce and evaporated milk; pour over casserole. Convection Bake at 325°F. for 35 to 40 minutes.

**Makes 6 servings**

## Italian Haddock

2 tablespoons olive oil
1 tablespoon lemon juice
1 cup tomatoes, chopped
1½ cups fresh mushrooms, sliced
¼ cup onion, chopped
¼ cup green pepper, chopped
2 tablespoons fresh parsley, snipped
¾ teaspoon oregano
½ teaspoon seasoned salt
¼ teaspoon garlic powder
1 (16 oz.) pkg. frozen haddock fillets, thawed
Dash salt
Dash pepper

In skillet, combine olive oil, lemon juice, tomatoes, mushrooms, onion, green pepper, parsley, oregano, seasoned salt and garlic powder. Sauté mixture until onion is tender.

Place fish fillets in 2-quart oblong glass baking dish; sprinkle with salt and pepper. Spoon vegetable mixture over fillets. Convection Bake at 350°F. for 20 to 25 minutes or until fish flakes easily.

**Makes 4 to 6 servings**

## Shrimp Enchiladas

½ cup sweet red pepper, chopped
½ cup onion, minced
½ cup green pepper, chopped
¼ cup butter
½ teaspoon oregano
½ teaspoon salt
¼ teaspoon garlic powder
⅛ teaspoon pepper
⅛ teaspoon cayenne pepper
¾ cup whipping cream
1 tablespoon all-purpose flour
3 cups Monterey Jack cheese, divided
½ cup sour cream
¼ cup butter, melted
1 lb. medium shrimp, uncooked, peeled and deveined
1 cup onion, chopped and divided
2 cups tomatoes, peeled and chopped, divided
8 (9-inch) flour tortillas

Sauté red pepper, onion and green pepper in ¼ cup butter until crisp-tender. Add oregano, salt, garlic powder, pepper, cayenne pepper, cream and flour; blend well. Continue cooking 3 minutes or until slightly thickened. Add 1½ cups cheese; stir until melted. Add sour cream, stir to blend. Set aside.

In medium bowl, place ¼ cup butter, shrimp and ½ cup onion. Microwave at HIGH (10) 4 to 5 minutes; stir after 2 minutes. Chop shrimp and return to butter and onion. Add 1 cup tomatoes and ½ of cheese sauce. Spoon ⅓ cup shrimp mixture into each tortilla. Roll up tightly. Arrange, seam side down, in 3-quart oblong glass baking dish. Spoon remaining cheese sauce over tortillas. Convection Bake at 350°F. for 30 to 35 minutes. Sprinkle enchiladas with remaining 1½ cups cheese, ½ cup onion and 1 cup tomatoes.

**Makes 4 servings**

*Spoon ⅓ cup of shrimp mixture onto each tortilla.*

*Roll up tightly and place seam side down in baking dish.*

# Casseroles

▲ *Vegetable Lasagna*

*Wear gloves when chopping hot peppers to protect from burning reaction.*

## Noodles Con Carne

½ **lb. ground beef**
½ **lb. hot bulk sausage**
½ **cup green pepper, chopped**
¼ **cup onion, chopped**
1 **hot pepper, chopped (optional)**
½ **teaspoon salt**
⅛ **teaspoon pepper**
1 **(15 oz.) can chili beans**
1 **(8 oz.) can tomato sauce**
1½ **tablespoons chili powder**
2 **cups Cheddar cheese, shredded**
6 **oz. wide egg noodles, cooked and drained**

Sauté ground beef, sausage, green pepper, onion, hot pepper, salt and pepper until meat is browned and onion is tender. Drain. Add chili beans, tomato sauce, chili powder, Cheddar cheese and egg noodles, mixing well. Convection Bake at 325°F. for 30 to 35 minutes or until hot.

**Makes 8 servings**

## Vegetable Lasagna

1 large onion, chopped
½ lb. carrots, shredded
½ lb. fresh mushrooms,
    coarsely chopped
2 tablespoons vegetable oil
2 cups small curd
    cottage cheese
2 eggs
¼ cup grated Parmesan
    cheese
1 teaspoon oregano
1 (15 ½ oz.) jar spaghetti
    sauce, divided
6 lasagna noodles, cooked
1 (10 oz.) pkg. frozen
    chopped spinach,
    thawed and drained
½ lb. tomatoes, peeled
    and coarsely chopped
2 cups mozzarella cheese,
    shredded

Sauté onion, carrots and mushrooms in oil over medium-high heat until tender. Drain and set aside. In small mixing bowl, combine cottage cheese, eggs, Parmesan cheese and oregano.

In 2-quart oblong glass baking dish, layer half of spaghetti sauce, 3 lasagna noodles, all onion-carrot-mushroom mixture and half of cheese mixture.

Cover with remaining noodles, spaghetti sauce, spinach and remaining cheese mixture. Top with tomatoes and mozzarella cheese. Convection Bake at 325°F. for 40 to 45 minutes. Let stand 10 minutes.

**Makes 6 servings**

*Spread half of cheese mixture over mixed vegetables to form first layer.*

*Form the second layer with remaining ingredients, starting with the noodles.*

## Italian Beef and Rice Casserole

1 lb. ground beef
1 cup onion, chopped
½ cup green pepper,
    chopped
½ cup celery, chopped
1 (14 ½ oz.) can tomatoes
1 (6 oz.) can Italian tomato
    paste
1 (4 oz.) can mushroom
    pieces, drained
2 tablespoons fresh
    parsley, snipped
1 teaspoon salt
½ teaspoon pepper
¼ teaspoon thyme
¼ teaspoon marjoram
1 cup rice, cooked
1 cup Cheddar cheese,
    shredded

Sauté beef, onion, green pepper and celery over medium-high heat until meat is browned and vegetables are tender. Drain. Add tomatoes, tomato paste, mushrooms, parsley, salt, pepper, thyme, marjoram and rice. Spoon mixture into 2-quart casserole. Convection Bake at 325°F. for 20 minutes. Top with cheese and continue baking 5 minutes or until cheese is melted.

**Makes 6 servings**

# Casseroles

## Chicken Pot Pie

3 whole chicken breasts,
   split and skinned
2 ½ cups water
Leaves from 2 stalks celery
1 ½ teaspoons salt
3 tablespoons vegetable oil
1 cup celery, chopped
½ cup green onion,
   chopped
⅓ cup all-purpose flour
1 (10 oz.) pkg. frozen peas
   and carrots, thawed
1 (2 oz.) jar sliced pimento
1 teaspoon thyme
½ teaspoon pepper
Pastry for 2 (9-inch)
   pie crusts

In 3-quart casserole, place chicken, water, celery leaves and salt. Microwave at HIGH (10) 14 to 17 minutes. Remove chicken breasts and celery leaves, reserving broth. Discard celery leaves. Cut chicken breasts into ½-inch cubes.

In 3-quart oblong glass baking dish, place oil, celery and green onion. Microwave at HIGH (10) 2 to 3 minutes until vegetables are crisp-tender. Stir in flour until smooth. Add chicken broth. Microwave at HIGH (10) 5 to 6 minutes, until thickened, stirring every 2 minutes. Add chicken, peas and carrots, pimento, thyme and pepper. Top with pie crust, crimping edges of crust around inside of dish. Decorate with pastry cut-outs if desired. Vent crust to allow steam to escape. Convection Bake at 425°F. for 20 to 25 minutes or until golden brown.

**Makes 8 servings**

## Lasagna

1 lb. ground beef
½ cup onion, chopped
2 (8 oz.) cans tomato sauce
1 (6 oz.) can tomato paste
¼ cup water
1 ¾ teaspoons basil
1 ½ teaspoons oregano
1 teaspoon parsley flakes
¾ teaspoon garlic salt
1 (12 oz.) carton small curd
   cottage cheese
1 egg, beaten
¼ teaspoon seasoned salt
6 lasagna noodles, cooked
2 (6 oz.) pkgs. mozzarella
   cheese, sliced
½ cup grated Parmesan
   cheese

Sauté beef and onion over medium-high heat until meat is browned; drain. Stir in tomato sauce, tomato paste, water, basil, oregano, parsley flakes and garlic salt. Set aside.

In small mixing bowl, combine cottage cheese, egg and seasoned salt.

In 2-quart oblong glass baking dish, spread ⅓ of meat sauce over bottom. Top with half of lasagna noodles, half of cottage cheese mixture and half of mozzarella cheese. Repeat layers, ending with meat sauce; sprinkle with Parmesan cheese. Convection Bake at 350°F. for 35 to 40 minutes.

**Makes 6 servings**

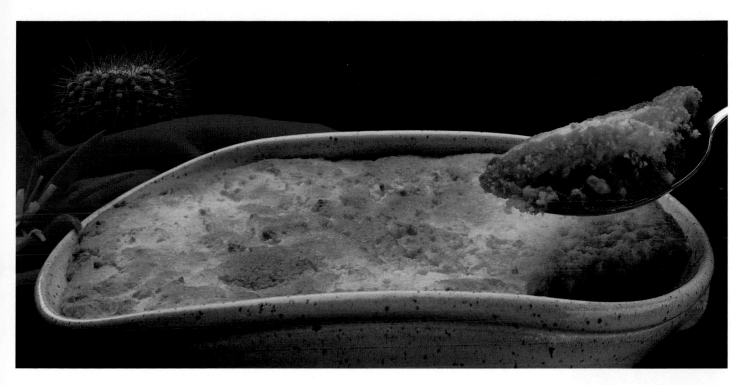

▲ *Tamale Pie*

## *Tamale Pie*

1 lb. ground beef
¼ lb. bulk pork sausage
¼ cup onion, chopped
⅛ teaspoon garlic powder
1 (16 oz.) can stewed
  tomatoes, drained
1 (17 oz.) can whole kernel
  corn, drained
1 (6 oz.) can tomato paste
2 teaspoons chili powder
1 teaspoon salt
⅓ cup pitted ripe olives,
  sliced
1 (8 ½ oz.) pkg. corn
  muffin mix
1 egg
⅓ cup milk
½ cup Cheddar cheese,
  shredded
Dash paprika

Sauté beef, sausage, onion and garlic over medium-high heat until meat is browned. Drain. Stir in tomatoes, corn, tomato paste, chili powder, salt and olives. Spoon mixture into 8-inch square baking dish.

In small mixing bowl, combine corn muffin mix, egg and milk just until moistened. Spread corn muffin mixture over meat mixture.

Convection Bake at 350°F. for 20 to 25 minutes or until center is set. Sprinkle with cheese and paprika; continue baking for 5 minutes or until cheese melts.

**Makes 4 to 6 servings**

*Evenly spread corn muffin mixture over beef mixture and bake.*

# Casseroles

▲ *Simple Tuna Casserole*

*Toss bread cubes in melted butter until coated evenly.*

## Simple Tuna Casserole

**3 tablespoons butter**
**2 tablespoons onion, chopped**
**3 tablespoons all-purpose flour**
**1 teaspoon salt**
**¼ teaspoon pepper**
**1½ cups milk**
**2 (6½ oz.) cans tuna, drained**
**2 cups soft bread cubes**
**2 tablespoons butter, melted**
**1 (10 oz.) pkg. frozen peas, cooked and drained**
**1 medium carrot, shredded**
**1 cup sharp Cheddar cheese, shredded**

In 2-quart casserole, place 3 tablespoons butter and onion. Microwave at HIGH (10) 2 to 3 minutes or until onion is transparent. Add flour, salt, pepper and milk. Stir well to blend. Microwave at HIGH (10) 5 to 6 minutes, until thickened, stirring every 2 minutes. Add tuna.

In 8-inch square glass baking dish, toss bread cubes in 2 tablespoons melted butter. Add peas and shredded carrot. Pour cream sauce over vegetables and top with cheese. Convection Bake at 325°F. for 20 to 25 minutes.

**Makes 4 servings**

## Hamburger & Zucchini Casserole

**1½ lbs. ground chuck**
**1 medium onion, chopped**
**1 (16 oz.) can whole kernel corn, drained**
**1 (14½ oz.) can tomatoes**
**1 (15 oz.) can tomato sauce**
**3 small zucchini, diced, cooked and drained**
**½ teaspoon garlic powder**
**½ teaspoon salt**
**¼ teaspoon pepper**

Sauté beef and onion over medium-high heat until meat is browned. Drain. Add corn, tomatoes, tomato sauce, zucchini, garlic powder, salt and pepper. Stir well. Spoon mixture into 3-quart casserole. Cover. Convection Bake at 325°F. for 25 to 30 minutes. Let stand, covered, 5 minutes before serving.

**Makes 6 to 8 servings**

## Enchilada Casserole

2 lbs. ground beef
1 medium onion, chopped
2 (8 oz.) cans tomato sauce
1 (12 oz.) can Mexicorn,
  drained
½ cup ripe olives, sliced
1 (10 oz.) can hot
  enchilada sauce
½ teaspoon salt
½ teaspoon oregano
¼ teaspoon chili powder
¼ teaspoon pepper
12 corn tortillas, divided
2 cups Cheddar cheese,
  shredded, divided

Sauté beef and onion over medium-high heat until meat is browned. Drain. Add tomato sauce, corn, ripe olives, enchilada sauce, salt, oregano, chili powder and pepper. Stir well.

Place 6 tortillas on bottom of 3-quart oblong glass baking dish. Pour half of meat mixture over tortillas. Sprinkle 1 cup of cheese on top. Repeat layers. Convection Bake at 325°F. for 25 to 30 minutes.

**Makes 8 servings**

*Place 6 tortillas in dish to start first layer.*

## Cheesy Chicken Casserole

½ cup mushrooms, sliced
⅓ cup green pepper,
  chopped
¼ cup onion, chopped
¼ cup butter
6 tablespoons all-purpose
  flour
1 (13 ¾ oz.) can chicken
  broth
1 cup milk
½ teaspoon salt
⅛ teaspoon pepper
1 (8 oz.) pkg. medium egg
  noodles, cooked
3 (5 oz.) cans cooked
  chicken
1 cup Cheddar cheese,
  shredded

In 3-quart casserole, combine mushrooms, green pepper, onion and butter. Cover with vented plastic wrap. Microwave at HIGH (10) 4 to 6 minutes, until tender, stirring every 2 minutes. Add flour, chicken broth, milk, salt and pepper. Stir well. Microwave at HIGH (10) 4 to 6 minutes, stirring with wire whisk, every 2 minutes. Add noodles and chicken. Top with Cheddar cheese. Convection Bake at 325°F. for 20 to 25 minutes.

**Makes 6 servings**

*Sprinkle first layer with cheese and repeat layers.*

# Casseroles

▲ *Chicken Enchiladas*

## Chicken Enchiladas

**4 (5 oz.) cans cooked
 chicken**
**2 cups sour cream**
**1 (10 ¾ oz.) can cream of
 chicken soup**
**1 ½ cups Monterey Jack
 cheese, shredded**
**1 ½ cups Colby cheese,
 shredded**
**1 (4 oz.) can chopped
 green chilies, drained**
**2 tablespoons onion,
 chopped**
**¼ teaspoon pepper**
**10 (10-inch) flour tortillas**
**1 cup Colby cheese,
 shredded**

In large mixing bowl, combine chicken, sour cream, soup, 1 ½ cups Monterey Jack cheese, 1 ½ cups Colby cheese, green chilies, onion and pepper. Mix well. Place ½ cup of mixture on each tortilla; roll up and place seam side down in 3-quart oblong glass baking dish. Convection Bake at 350°F. for 20 to 25 minutes. Sprinkle with 1 cup Colby cheese and continue baking 5 minutes or until cheese is melted.

**Makes 5 servings**

## Turkey Tetrazzini

¼ cup butter, melted
¼ cup all-purpose flour
1 cup chicken broth
1 cup half & half
4 cups cooked turkey, cut up
1 (2 oz.) jar pimento, chopped
1 (7 oz.) pkg. spaghetti, cooked and drained
1 (4 oz.) can sliced mushrooms, drained
½ teaspoon salt
½ teaspoon pepper
¼ cup grated Parmesan cheese

In 4-cup glass measure, combine butter and flour. Gradually add broth and half & half, stirring until smooth. Microwave at MEDIUM HIGH (7) 5 to 6 minutes, until thickened, stirring every 2 minutes Combine sauce, turkey, pimento, spaghetti, mushrooms, salt and pepper; blend well. Spoon mixture into 3-quart oblong glass baking dish. Sprinkle Parmesan cheese over top. Convection Bake at 325°F. for 20 to 25 minutes.

**Makes 6 servings**

## Hearty Bean Casserole

1½ lbs. ground beef
1 (17 oz.) can lima beans, drained
1 (16 oz.) can pork and beans
1 (15½ oz.) can red kidney beans, drained
1 (8 oz.) can tomato sauce
⅓ cup onion, minced
½ cup catsup
¼ cup dark molasses
2 tablespoons vinegar
½ teaspoon salt
½ teaspoon dry mustard
½ teaspoon hot sauce

Sauté beef over medium-high heat until browned. Drain. Add lima beans, pork and beans, kidney beans, tomato sauce, onion, catsup, molasses, vinegar, salt, dry mustard and hot sauce; stir to combine. Spoon mixture into 3-quart casserole. Convection Bake at 350°F. for 30 to 35 minutes or until bubbly.

**Makes 8 servings**

## Spicy Wild Rice Casserole

1 lb. hot bulk sausage
½ cup celery, chopped
½ cup onion, chopped
½ cup mushrooms, sliced
½ cup green pepper, chopped
1½ cups water
1 (10¾ oz.) can cream of mushroom soup
1 (6 oz.) pkg. long grain and wild rice with seasoning packet
1 cup Cheddar cheese, shredded

Sauté sausage, celery, onion, mushrooms and green pepper over medium-high heat until meat is browned and vegetables are tender. Drain. Add water, soup, rice and cheese. Spoon mixture into 2-quart oblong glass baking dish. Convection Bake at 300°F. for 55 to 60 minutes.

**Makes 6 to 8 servings**

# Eggs & Cheese

▲ *Asparagus Egg Roll-Up With Cheese Sauce*

## Asparagus Egg Roll-Up With Cheese Sauce

*Invert from jelly roll pan onto wax paper.*

**1 (10 oz.) pkg. frozen asparagus spears, cooked and drained**
**6 tablespoons butter, melted**
**¾ cup all-purpose flour**
**1 teaspoon dry mustard**
**½ teaspoon salt**
**3 cups milk**
**4 eggs, separated**
**⅓ cup half & half**
**1 cup Swiss cheese, shredded**

Grease and flour a 15x10x1-inch jelly roll pan. Line pan with wax paper, allowing paper to extend beyond the ends of the pan. Grease the wax paper with vegetable shortening, and dust lightly with flour. Set aside. Cut asparagus into ½-inch pieces. Set aside. In saucepan, melt butter, stir in flour, dry mustard and salt. Add milk. Cook over medium heat until thickened and bubbly, stirring constantly. Cook and stir 1 minute longer. Set aside 1 cup of white sauce mixture.

Place egg yolks in large mixing bowl and beat slightly. Gradually blend in remaining white sauce mixture. In medium bowl, beat egg whites at high speed until stiff peaks form. Fold egg whites into egg yolk mixture. Spoon mixture into jelly roll pan, spreading evenly. Convection Bake at 300°F. for 40 to 45 minutes until puffed and firm. Loosen edges around pan. Invert jelly roll pan on wax paper. Remove pan; peel off wax paper.

Return 1 cup reserved sauce to saucepan. Add half & half and cheese. Cook over low heat until cheese is melted and sauce is smooth, stirring constantly. Spread ¾ cup cheese sauce over roll. Top with asparagus. Starting at narrow end, carefully roll into jelly roll, using wax paper for support. Top with remaining cheese sauce.

**Makes 8 servings**

## *Corn and Cheese Souffle*

¼ cup butter, melted
¼ cup all-purpose flour
¼ teaspoon salt
⅛ teaspoon white pepper
1½ cups milk
2 ¼ cups Cheddar cheese, shredded
1 (8 oz.) can whole kernel corn, drained
6 eggs, separated

In 1½-quart casserole, combine melted butter, flour, salt and pepper. Gradually stir in milk. Microwave at MEDIUM HIGH (7) 4 to 6 minutes, until slightly thickened, stirring every 2 minutes. Add cheese and corn. Microwave at MEDIUM HIGH (7) 2 minutes; stir to blend. In small mixing bowl, beat egg yolks. Stir in a small amount of cheese sauce; return yolk mixture to sauce, blending well. Cool slightly.

In medium mixing bowl, beat egg whites until soft peaks form. With a rubber spatula, fold egg whites into cheese sauce just until blended. Pour into greased 2-quart souffle dish. Convection Bake at 325°F. for 35 to 40 minutes or until top is puffed and golden and center is set. Serve immediately.

**Makes 4 servings**

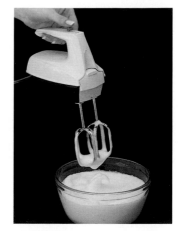

*Beat egg whites until soft peaks form.*

## *Pepper Cheese Pastry*

1 medium onion, thinly sliced
½ cup sweet red pepper, cut into 2-inch thin strips
½ cup green pepper, cut into 2-inch thin strips
2 tablespoons olive oil
½ teaspoon hot sauce
2 (8 oz.) pkgs. crescent rolls
½ cup grated Parmesan cheese
1 lb. Monterey Jack cheese, shredded

Sauté onion, red pepper and green pepper in oil until crisp-tender. Stir in hot sauce. Set aside. Grease a 15x10x1-inch jelly roll pan. Press crescent roll dough onto jelly roll pan. Convection Bake at 325°F. for 5 minutes. Sprinkle with Parmesan cheese. Top with onion mixture and Monterey Jack cheese. Continue baking for 15 minutes or until cheese begins to brown.

**Makes 8 servings**

*Gently fold egg whites into cheese sauce to blend.*

## *Macaroni & Cheese*

1 (7 oz.) pkg. elbow macaroni
2 cups sharp Cheddar cheese, shredded
2 tablespoons butter
2 cups milk
1 teaspoon Worcestershire sauce
2 tablespoons all-purpose flour
1 teaspoon salt
⅛ teaspoon pepper

Cook macaroni according to package directions; drain. In lightly greased 2-quart casserole, combine macaroni, cheese and butter. Combine milk, Worcestershire sauce, flour, salt and pepper; stir to blend. Pour over macaroni mixture. Convection Bake at 350°F. for 35 to 40 minutes.

**Makes 6 servings**

# Eggs & Cheese

▲ *Vegetable Frittata*

## Vegetable Frittata

**2 tablespoons butter**
**1 small onion, sliced**
**4 asparagus tips, sliced**
**3 mushrooms, sliced**
**½ small zucchini, sliced**
**8 eggs, beaten**
**½ cup milk**
**¼ teaspoon salt**
**⅛ teaspoon pepper**
**Dash hot sauce**

Place butter and onion in 9-inch quiche dish. Microwave at HIGH (10) 2 to 3 minutes. Add asparagus, mushrooms and zucchini. Microwave at HIGH (10) 4 to 5 minutes; stir after 2 minutes. In small mixing bowl, combine eggs, milk, salt, pepper and hot sauce. Pour over vegetables. Convection Bake at 325°F. for 25 to 30 minutes or until set.

**Makes 4 servings**

## Breakfast Cheese Pizza

*Arrange sliced bread buttered side down to form crust.*

**3 green onions, chopped**
**½ cup fresh mushrooms,**
 **finely chopped**
**1 tablespoon bacon**
 **drippings**
**5 slices bread, buttered**
**Garlic salt**
**1 cup Cheddar cheese,**
 **shredded**
**1 cup Swiss cheese,**
 **shredded**
**2 tablespoons all-purpose**
 **flour**
**6 slices bacon, cooked**
 **and crumbled**
**1½ cups milk**
**2 eggs**
**¼ teaspoon salt**
**¼ teaspoon pepper**

Sauté onions and mushrooms in bacon drippings until onions are transparent and mushrooms are tender. Set aside. Sprinkle buttered bread with garlic salt. Cut slices in half diagonally. Arrange, buttered side down, in 10-inch pie plate, forming a crust. Sprinkle onions and mushrooms over bread.

Combine Cheddar cheese, Swiss cheese, flour and bacon. Spread over top of onions and mushrooms. In small mixing bowl, beat together milk, eggs, salt and pepper. Pour evenly over cheese. Convection Bake at 325°F. for 35 to 40 minutes or until knife inserted in center comes out clean.

**Makes 6 to 8 servings**

## Spinach Quiche

1 ¾ cups fresh mushrooms, sliced
1 tablespoon butter
1 (12 oz.) pkg. frozen spinach souffle, thawed
½ lb. sweet Italian sausage, cooked and crumbled
¾ cup Swiss cheese, shredded
2 eggs, beaten
3 tablespoons whipping cream
½ teaspoon pepper
½ teaspoon hot sauce
1 (9-inch) deep-dish pie crust, baked

Sauté mushrooms in butter until tender; drain well. Add spinach souffle, sausage, cheese, eggs, cream, pepper and hot sauce. Pour into crust. Convection Bake at 325°F. for 35 to 40 minutes or until knife inserted in center comes out clean. Let stand 10 minutes before serving.

**Makes 6 servings**

*Test for doneness by inserting knife in center. Knife should come out clean.*

## Ham & Grits Quiche

½ cup fresh mushrooms, chopped
¼ cup onion, chopped
1 tablespoon butter
½ cup milk
½ cup whipping cream
4 eggs, beaten
½ teaspoon dry mustard
¼ teaspoon pepper
¼ teaspoon nutmeg
½ cup Swiss cheese, shredded
½ cup Cheddar cheese, shredded
¾ cup cooked ham, chopped
4 sausage links, chopped and cooked
1 (9-inch) deep dish pie crust, baked
3 bacon slices, chopped and cooked
½ cup quick cooking grits, cooked

Sauté mushrooms and onion in butter until tender. Set aside. In medium mixing bowl, combine milk, whipping cream, eggs, dry mustard, pepper and nutmeg. Set aside.

In separate mixing bowl, combine Swiss cheese and Cheddar cheese. Sprinkle ham and sausage over bottom of crust. Top with half of cheese and all of bacon. Spread mushroom mixture over bacon. Add grits. Sprinkle with remaining cheese. Pour cream mixture over cheese. Convection Bake at 325°F. for 45 to 50 minutes or until knife inserted in center comes out clean. Let stand 10 minutes before serving.

**Makes 6 servings**

# Eggs & Cheese

▲ *Ham and Egg Casserole*

## *Ham and Egg Casserole*

**3 cups white bread cubes,
    crusts removed**
**2 cups sharp Cheddar
    cheese, shredded**
**¼  cup green onion,
    finely chopped**
**1 (4 ½  oz.) can sliced
    mushrooms, drained**
**1 cup ham, cut into
    ½ -inch cubes**
**4 eggs**
**½  cup milk**
**1 teaspoon dry mustard**
**⅛  teaspoon pepper**
**Dash hot sauce**

In 2-quart oblong glass baking dish, place cubed bread.
Sprinkle cheese, green onion and mushrooms over
bread. Top with ham cubes. In small mixing bowl, beat
together eggs, milk, dry mustard, pepper and hot sauce.
Pour egg mixture over bread, cheese and ham.
Convection Bake at 325°F. for 35 to 40 minutes or until
knife inserted in center comes out clean.

**Makes 4 to 6 servings**

## Garlic Cheese and Grits Casserole

3 cups hot tap water
¾ cup quick cooking grits
¾ teaspoon salt
5 tablespoons butter, sliced
1½ cups sharp Cheddar cheese, shredded
2 eggs
Milk
¼ teaspoon garlic powder
Dash hot sauce
½ cup sharp Cheddar cheese, shredded
Paprika

In 3-quart casserole, place water, grits and salt. Microwave at HIGH (10) 10 to 12 minutes; stir after 5 minutes. Add butter and 1½ cups cheese to grits. Stir well until melted. Beat eggs; add enough milk to total ¾ cup. Add garlic powder and hot sauce. Quickly stir into grits. Pour into well-greased 8-inch square baking dish. Sprinkle ½ cup cheese over top. Sprinkle with paprika. Convection Bake at 325°F. for 40 to 45 minutes or until knife inserted in center comes out clean.

**Makes 6 servings**

## Cheese-Stuffed Manicotti

2 cups mozzarella cheese, shredded, divided
2 cups ricotta cheese
½ cup Romano cheese
1 (7 ¾ oz.) can spinach, drained
½ teaspoon garlic powder
½ teaspoon salt
¼ teaspoon pepper
10 manicotti, cooked
1 (15 oz.) can tomato sauce
⅛ teaspoon sweet basil
⅛ teaspoon oregano

In medium mixing bowl, combine 1 cup mozzarella, ricotta, Romano, spinach, garlic powder, salt and pepper. Stuff cooked manicotti with cheese filling. Arrange in 2-quart oblong glass baking dish. Set aside. Combine tomato sauce, basil and oregano. Pour over manicotti. Sprinkle with remaining mozzarella. Convection Bake at 350°F. for 30 to 35 minutes.

**Makes 5 servings**

*Stuff cooked manicotti with cheese filling.*

# Vegetables

▲ *Stuffed Yellow Squash*

*Scoop out pulp and seeds leaving ¼-inch thick shell.*

## Stuffed Yellow Squash

**3 large yellow squash**
**¼ lb. hot bulk sausage**
**½ cup green pepper, chopped**
**¼ cup onion, chopped**
**1 medium tomato, chopped**
**½ cup grated Parmesan cheese**
**1 cup mozzarella cheese, shredded**

Cut squash in half, lengthwise. Scoop out pulp and seeds; discard, leaving ¼-inch thick shell. Set aside. Sauté sausage, green pepper and onion over medium-high heat until meat is browned. Drain. Add tomato and Parmesan cheese. Stir until well blended.

Divide sausage mixture evenly among squash shells; place squash in 3-quart oblong glass baking dish. Cover with aluminum foil. Convection Bake at 325°F. for 20 minutes. Remove foil. Sprinkle with cheese and continue baking 5 minutes or until cheese is melted.

**Makes 6 servings**

## Asparagus and Cheese Brunch

8 slices bread
1 (16 oz.) can asparagus, drained, cut into 2-inch pieces
2 cups Cheddar cheese, shredded
4 eggs, beaten
2 cups milk
2 tablespoons onion, minced
1½ teaspoons salt
¼ teaspoon dry mustard
¼ teaspoon paprika
⅛ teaspoon pepper

Remove crusts from bread and cut into cubes. In 2-quart oblong glass baking dish, arrange half the bread. Cover with asparagus and sprinkle with Cheddar cheese. Cover with remaining bread. Combine eggs, milk, onion, salt, mustard, paprika and pepper. Pour mixture over casserole. Let stand 20 minutes. Convection Bake at 300°F. for 45 to 50 minutes or until puffed and lightly browned. Let stand 5 minutes.

**Makes 6 servings**

## Corn Pudding

2 tablespoons butter, melted
2 tablespoons all-purpose flour
2 tablespoons sugar
½ teaspoon salt
1 cup milk
3 eggs, beaten
1 (16 oz.) can whole kernel corn, drained

In 1½-quart casserole, combine butter, flour, sugar, salt, milk, eggs and corn. Convection Bake at 325°F. for 30 to 35 minutes or until center is barely set.

**Makes 4 to 6 servings**

## Parmesan Cheese Potato Slices

3 large baking potatoes, sliced ¼-inch thick
½ cup grated Parmesan cheese
⅛ teaspoon paprika
3 tablespoons butter, melted

Place sliced potatoes on baking sheet. Combine Parmesan cheese and paprika. Brush potato slices with butter and sprinkle with Parmesan cheese mixture. Convection Bake at 350°F. for 25 to 30 minutes.

**Makes 6 servings**

# Vegetables

## Acorn Squash with Cranberry Filling

2 medium acorn squash
(about 2 lbs.)
1 (16 oz.) can whole berry
cranberry sauce
1 tablespoon honey
¼ teaspoon allspice

Prick squash several times with fork to allow steam to escape. Microwave at HIGH (10) 16 to 22 minutes until soft when pricked with fork. Turn squash over and rearrange after 9 minutes. Let stand 5 minutes. Cut in half and remove seeds. Place cut side up in 10-in. pie plate.

In small bowl, combine cranberry sauce, honey and allspice. Spoon into squash halves. Convection Bake at 325°F. for 15 to 20 minutes or until filling is hot.

**Makes 4 servings**

## Delicious Yams

1 (30 oz.) can yams,
well drained
⅓ cup orange juice
1 tablespoon cornstarch
½ cup brown sugar,
firmly packed
¼ cup butter, melted
½ cup walnuts, coarsely
chopped
1½ cups miniature
marshmallows

Arrange yams in 1½-quart casserole. In medium bowl, combine orange juice and cornstarch; stir until cornstarch is completely dissolved. Blend in brown sugar and butter. Add walnuts and pour over yams. Convection Bake at 350°F. for 20 minutes. Arrange marshmallows on top and continue baking for 5 to 10 minutes or until lightly browned.

**Makes 6 servings**

## Scalloped Potatoes

¼ cup butter, melted
¼ cup all-purpose flour
2 cups milk
1 tablespoon dried onion
flakes
1 teaspoon salt
¼ teaspoon pepper
6 medium potatoes,
peeled and thinly sliced
Paprika

In 4-cup glass measure, combine melted butter and flour; gradually add milk, stirring until smooth. Add onion flakes, salt and pepper. Microwave at MEDIUM-HIGH (7) 7 to 9 minutes, until sauce is smooth and slightly thickened, stirring every 3 minutes. In 2-quart casserole, alternately layer potatoes and sauce. Cover. Convection Bake at 325°F. for 30 minutes. Uncover and continue baking 30 minutes or until tender. Let stand 5 minutes.

**Makes 6 servings**

▲ *Cabbage Rolls*

# Cabbage Rolls

**8 whole, fresh cabbage
   leaves**
**½ cup water**
**1 lb. ground chuck**
**½ cup instant rice**
**3 tablespoons onion,
   finely chopped**
**3 tablespoons green
   pepper, finely chopped**
**1 teaspoon salt**
**⅛ teaspoon pepper**
**⅛ teaspoon nutmeg**
**½ cup tomato juice**
**1 (15 oz.) can tomato sauce**
**3 tablespoons brown
   sugar, firmly packed**
**1 tablespoon lemon juice**
**1 tablespoon
   Worcestershire sauce**
**½ teaspoon garlic salt**

In 3-quart casserole, place cabbage leaves and water. Cover. Microwave at HIGH (10) 7 to 9 minutes until leaves are soft and pliable. Drain. In medium size mixing bowl, combine ground chuck, rice, onion, green pepper, salt, pepper and nutmeg. Divide into 8 portions and place one portion on each of the partially-cooked cabbage leaves. Roll leaf around meat mixture. Secure with a toothpick. Place rolls, seam-side down in 3-quart casserole.

Combine tomato juice, tomato sauce, brown sugar, lemon juice, Worcestershire sauce and garlic salt. Pour over cabbage rolls. Cover. Convection Bake at 325°F. for 40 to 45 minutes. Baste rolls with sauce every 15 minutes.

**Makes 4 servings**

*Cooked cabbage leaves should be soft and pliable.*

*Wrap leaf around meat mixture and secure with toothpick.*

# Vegetables

## Southern Stuffed Eggplant

*Scoop out eggplant leaving the outer shell intact and dice the insides to be used in the stuffing.*

1 medium eggplant
2 tablespoons water
¼ cup chopped onion
2 teaspoons parsley, snipped
2 tablespoons butter
1 (10 ½ oz.) can condensed cream of mushroom soup
¼ teaspoon salt
⅛ teaspoon pepper
1 teaspoon Worcestershire sauce
¾ cup butter cracker crumbs, divided
½ cup salted peanuts, coarsely chopped, optional
Paprika

Cut eggplant in half lengthwise. Scoop out pulp leaving outer shell intact. Dice the scooped-out eggplant. In 2-quart casserole, combine diced eggplant and water. Cover. Microwave at HIGH (10) 6 to 8 minutes; stir after 3 minutes. Drain.

Sauté onion and parsley in butter until onion is transparent.

Combine onion mixture, soup, salt, pepper, Worcestershire sauce, ½ cup cracker crumbs, peanuts and eggplant pieces. Evenly divide filling between the 2 shells. Place in 2-quart oblong glass baking dish. Convection Bake at 325°F. for 40 minutes. Sprinkle ¼ cup crumbs and paprika over top. Continue baking 5 minutes.

**Makes 4 servings**

## Cheesy Broccoli

1 cup instant rice
1 (10 ¾ oz.) can condensed cream of chicken soup
½ cup milk
1 (8 oz.) jar processed cheese spread
¼ teaspoon pepper
1 (10 oz.) pkg. frozen chopped broccoli, cooked and drained
½ cup celery, chopped
¼ cup onion, chopped

In 2-quart casserole, combine rice, soup, milk, cheese and pepper. Microwave at HIGH (10) 2 to 4 minutes until cheese melts and can be blended easily.

To cheese mixture, add broccoli, celery and onion. Stir thoroughly. Convection Bake at 325°F. for 25 to 30 minutes or until bubbly.

**Makes 6 servings**

## Twice-Baked Potatoes

2 large baking potatoes
2 tablespoons butter
¼ cup milk
½ teaspoon salt
¼ teaspoon garlic powder
⅛ teaspoon pepper
½ cup Cheddar cheese, shredded

Scrub potatoes thoroughly with a brush. Pat dry. Prick skins with a fork. Convection Bake at 400°F. for 45 to 50 minutes.

Cut cooked potatoes in half. Scoop out potatoes leaving ¼-inch thick shell. Set aside. In a medium mixing bowl, combine scooped out potato, butter, milk, salt, garlic powder and pepper. Whip potatoes with electric mixer at high speed for 1 minute or until smooth.

In an 8-inch square glass baking dish, place potato shells and fill with whipped potato mixture. Sprinkle Cheddar cheese on top. Convection Bake at 400°F. for 20 minutes or until heated through.

**Makes 2 servings**

## Spinach with Artichokes Casserole

1 (8 oz.) pkg. cream cheese,
softened
4 tablespoons butter,
softened
2 tablespoons mayonnaise
6 tablespoons milk
1 (14 oz.) can artichoke
hearts, drained
2 (10 oz.) pkgs. frozen
chopped spinach,
thawed and drained
⅓ cup grated Parmesan
cheese
Dash pepper

In medium mixing bowl, combine cream cheese, butter and mayonnaise. Beat with an electric mixer for 2 minutes until light and fluffy. Gradually beat in milk.

In 2-quart casserole, place artichokes. Spoon spinach evenly over artichokes. Spread cream cheese mixture over spinach. Sprinkle with Parmesan cheese and pepper. Convection Bake at 350°F. for 20 to 25 minutes or until top is lightly browned.

**Makes 6 to 8 servings**

*Drain spinach thoroughly before adding to the artichokes.*

## Three Bean Bake

⅓ cup red onion, chopped
¼ lb. bacon, cooked and
crumbled, reserve
drippings
¼ cup brown sugar,
firmly packed
1 tablespoon cider vinegar
1 teaspoon dry mustard
½ teaspoon salt
1 (16 oz.) can pork & beans
1 (15½ oz.) can kidney
beans, drained
1 (17 oz.) can lima beans,
drained

Sauté onion in bacon drippings until tender. Combine sauteed onion, brown sugar, vinegar, mustard, salt, pork and beans, kidney beans, lima beans and crumbled bacon in 2-quart oblong glass baking dish. Stir well. Convection Bake at 350°F. for 25 to 30 minutes or until bubbly.

**Makes 6 to 8 servings**

## Yellow Squash Casserole

6 yellow squash,
coarsely chopped
½ cup water
1 dozen round buttery
crackers
1 (3 oz.) pkg. cream
cheese, softened
1 (10¾ oz.) can cream of
chicken soup
1 egg
¼ cup butter, melted
3 small carrots, grated
½ cup onion,
finely chopped
½ cup herb-seasoned
stuffing mix

In 2-quart casserole, combine squash and water. Cover. Microwave at HIGH (10) 10 minutes; stir after 5 minutes. Drain well and set aside.

Place crackers in greased 2-quart oblong glass baking dish. In medium mixing bowl, combine cream cheese, soup, egg and butter. Beat with electric mixer at high speed for 1 minute. Stir in squash, carrots and onion. Spoon into cracker-lined baking dish; sprinkle with stuffing mix. Convection Bake at 325°F. for 25 to 30 minutes or until bubbly.

**Makes 10 to 12 servings**

# Breads

▲ *Banana Muffins*

## Banana Muffins

**3 cups all-purpose flour**
**1½ cups pecans,**
**coarsely chopped**
**1 cup oats, uncooked**
**1 cup corn flakes**
**1 tablespoon baking**
**powder**
**2 teaspoons baking soda**
**½ teaspoon salt**
**4 large ripe bananas,**
**mashed (2 cups)**
**1 cup milk**
**1 cup honey**
**4 tablespoons butter,**
**melted**
**1 egg**

In large mixing bowl, combine flour, pecans, oats, corn flakes, baking powder, baking soda and salt. In medium mixing bowl, beat together bananas, milk, honey, butter and egg. Add banana mixture to dry ingredients; stir until moistened. Spoon batter into paper-lined muffin pans. Convection Bake at 375°F. for 13 to 16 minutes or until golden brown.

**Makes 24 muffins**

## Spicy Corn Muffins

1 cup self-rising corn meal
½ cup all-purpose flour
1 teaspoon chili powder
½ teaspoon salt
2 tablespoons onion,
   finely chopped
¾ cup buttermilk
2 eggs, beaten
2 tablespoons honey
2 tablespoons vegetable oil
1 cup French-fried onions,
   finely crushed

In medium mixing bowl, sift together corn meal, flour, chili powder and salt. Add onion, buttermilk, eggs, honey and oil. Spoon batter into well-greased muffin pan, filling each cup ½ full. Sprinkle French-fried onions over top. Convection Bake at 375°F. for 12 to 15 minutes.

**Makes 10 to 12 muffins**

## Orange-Nut Muffins

2 cups all-purpose flour
⅓ cup sugar
1 teaspoon baking powder
½ teaspoon baking soda
¼ teaspoon salt
1 cup natural nutty cereal
¾ cup raisins
¾ cup orange juice
⅓ cup vegetable oil
1½ teaspoons grated
   orange rind

In large mixing bowl, combine flour, sugar, baking powder, baking soda, salt, cereal and raisins. Combine orange juice, oil and orange rind; add to dry ingredients. Blend until moistened. Spoon batter into well-greased muffin pan, filling each cup ½ full. Convection Bake at 375°F. for 13 to 16 minutes.

**Makes 15 to 18 muffins**

## Old Fashioned Biscuits

2 cups all-purpose flour
⅓ cup sugar
2 teaspoons baking
   powder
½ teaspoon baking soda
¼ teaspoon salt
¼ cup butter
1 cup whipping cream

Preheat oven to 400°F.
In large mixing bowl, combine flour, sugar, baking powder, baking soda and salt. Using a pastry blender, cut in butter until mixture resembles coarse crumbs. Add cream. Stir until mixture forms stiff dough. Turn dough onto lightly floured surface. Knead to mix thoroughly. Roll out dough to ½-inch thickness. Using a floured 2-inch biscuit cutter, cut out biscuits. Place on ungreased cookie sheet, 1-inch apart. Convection Bake at 400°F. for 6 to 8 minutes or until biscuits are golden brown.

**Makes 20 biscuits**

# Breads

## Zucchini Bread

1¾ cups all-purpose flour
1 teaspoon cinnamon
1 teaspoon baking soda
½ teaspoon salt
1 cup sugar
1 cup zucchini, grated
2 eggs
½ cup vegetable oil
½ cup plain yogurt
1½ teaspoons vanilla
1 cup pecans, chopped

In small mixing bowl, sift together flour, cinnamon, baking soda and salt. In medium mixing bowl, combine sugar, zucchini, eggs, oil, yogurt and vanilla. Add flour mixture; stir well. Fold in nuts. Pour batter into well-greased and floured 9x5x3-inch loaf pan. Convection Bake at 325°F. for 55 to 60 minutes or until toothpick inserted in center comes out clean. Remove from pan and let cool on wire rack.

**Makes 1 (9-inch) loaf**

## Banana Bread

¾ cup sugar
½ cup butter
¾ cup mashed bananas
   (about 2 medium)
2 teaspoons lemon juice
⅓ cup milk
2 eggs, beaten
1½ cups all-purpose flour
1 teaspoon baking soda
½ teaspoon baking
   powder
½ cup walnuts, chopped

Grease a 9x5x3-inch loaf pan; set aside. In large mixer bowl, cream sugar and butter with an electric mixer. Mix in mashed bananas and lemon juice; add milk and eggs. Sift in flour, baking soda and baking powder. Blend well. Stir in nuts. Pour into prepared pan. Convection Bake at 325°F. for 35 to 40 minutes.

**Makes 1 (9-inch) loaf**

## Oatmeal-Orange Coffee Cake

1½ cups all-purpose flour
1 cup oats, uncooked
⅓ cup brown sugar,
   firmly packed
1 tablespoon baking
   powder
½ teaspoon baking soda
2 ripe bananas, mashed
½ cup orange juice
⅓ cup butter, melted
1 egg, beaten
¼ teaspoon orange rind,
   grated
½ teaspoon vanilla
½ cup powdered sugar
1 tablespoon orange juice
¼ teaspoon orange rind,
   grated

In large mixing bowl, combine flour, oats, brown sugar, baking powder and baking soda. Combine bananas, orange juice, butter, egg, ¼ teaspoon orange rind and vanilla. Add to flour mixture. Mix until moistened. Grease the bottom of a 9-inch round springform pan. Pour batter into pan. Convection Bake at 350°F. for 25 to 30 minutes or until golden brown. Cool 10 minutes on wire rack; remove from pan.

In small mixing bowl, combine powdered sugar, orange juice and remaining orange rind. Drizzle evenly over cake while still warm.

**Makes 1 (9-inch) coffee cake**

▲ *Toasted Coconut Pretzels*

## Toasted Coconut Pretzels

**3 cups all-purpose flour**
**½ cup butter, sliced**
**1 ( ¼ oz.) pkg. dry yeast**
**¼ cup granulated sugar,**
**    divided**
**¼ cup warm water**
**1 cup whipping cream**
**3 egg yolks, beaten**
**½ teaspoon salt**

***Topping:***
**1 egg white**
**1 cup coconut, toasted**
**½ cup brown sugar,**
**    firmly packed**

Place flour in large mixing bowl. Cut in butter, with a pastry blender, until mixture resembles coarse crumbs. Cover and refrigerate. Sprinkle yeast and 1 tablespoon of granulated sugar over warm water in medium mixing bowl; stir to dissolve. Let stand 5 minutes until foamy. Add cream, egg yolks, salt and remaining sugar; stir well. Pour over flour mixture and stir until flour is just moistened. Cover and refrigerate dough at least 12 hours.

Punch dough down. Roll out on lightly floured surface into 16-inch square. Fold dough over into thirds. Starting on the short side, roll dough out into approximately 10x20-inch rectangle. With pizza cutter, cut 10-inch strips approximately ¾-inch wide. Form each strip into a pretzel shape. Brush each pretzel with egg white. In small mixing bowl, combine coconut and brown sugar; sprinkle coconut mixture on top of each pretzel. Convection Bake at 325°F. for 15 to 17 minutes.

**Makes 20 to 25 pretzels**

*With pizza cutter, cut 10-inch strips approximately ¾-inch wide.*

*Form each strip into a pretzel shape. Pinch ends to seal.*

# Breads

## Sour Cream Bread

2 cups all-purpose flour
1 cup sugar
1½ teaspoons baking
  powder
1 teaspoon baking soda
½ cup butter
1 (8 oz.) container
  sour cream
3 eggs, beaten
2½ teaspoons vanilla
¼ teaspoon almond
  extract
¾ cup pecans, chopped

### Crumb Topping:
⅔ cup all-purpose flour
⅓ cup sugar
⅓ cup butter

Grease a 9x5x3-inch loaf pan; set aside.

In large mixing bowl, combine 2 cups flour, 1 cup sugar, baking powder and baking soda. Using a pastry blender, cut in butter until mixture resembles coarse crumbs. Blend in sour cream, eggs, vanilla and almond extract. Fold in pecans. Pour batter into prepared pan.

In small bowl, combine ⅔ cup flour and ⅓ cup sugar. Using a pastry blender, cut in butter until mixture resembles coarse crumbs. Sprinkle crumb topping over batter. Convection Bake at 325°F. for 55 to 65 minutes or until toothpick inserted in center comes out clean.

**Makes 10 servings**

*Arrange dough slices cut side down in bottom of pan. Space evenly.*

## Buttery Almond Crown

3 cups all-purpose flour
1¼ cups butter, sliced
2 (¼ oz.) pkgs. dry yeast
¼ cup sugar, divided
¼ cup warm water
½ cup evaporated milk
2 eggs, beaten
½ teaspoon salt
½ teaspoon butter
  flavoring

### Filling:
½ cup butter
½ cup sugar
½ cup almond paste
½ teaspoon almond
  extract
¼ cup sliced almonds,
  toasted

Place flour in large mixing bowl. Using a pastry blender, cut in butter until mixture resembles coarse crumbs. In medium mixing bowl, sprinkle yeast and 1 tablespoon of sugar over warm water; stir to dissolve. Let stand 5 minutes until foamy. Add milk, eggs, salt, butter flavoring and remaining sugar. Pour over flour mixture and stir until flour is just moistened. Cover and refrigerate at least 5 hours. Punch dough down. Roll out on lightly floured surface to 20-inch square. Fold dough into 3 equal portions. Starting at short end, roll out into 6½x30-inch rectangle. Fold dough into thirds again, forming a 6½x10-inch rectangle. Refrigerate. In medium mixing bowl, cream ½ cup butter, sugar, almond paste and almond extract with an electric mixer. Butter a 12-cup Bundt pan. Sprinkle bottom with almonds. Roll dough out on lightly floured surface into 9x24-inch rectangle. Spread filling on dough. Starting at long side, roll in jelly roll fashion. Cut dough crosswise into eight equal slices. Arrange slices cut side down in bottom of Bundt pan. Let rise in warm place about 1½ hours or until almost double in size. Convection Bake at 325°F. for 35 to 40 minutes or until top is golden brown. Cool on wire rack.

**Makes 12 servings**

*Cinnamon Bread* ▲

# Cinnamon Bread

⅓ cup sugar
1 tablespoon salt
½ cup shortening
1 cup milk, scalded
½ cup cold water
1 (¼ oz.) pkg. dry yeast
¼ cup warm water
1 egg, beaten
5 ½ to 6 cups all-purpose
  flour
2 tablespoons butter,
  softened
½ cup sugar
4 teaspoons cinnamon

In large mixing bowl, combine ⅓ cup sugar, salt, shortening and hot milk; stir until shortening melts. Add cold water. Dissolve yeast in warm water; add to milk mixture. Add egg; stir well. Add enough flour to form soft dough. Knead on floured surface 3 minutes until smooth. Place in large well-greased mixing bowl; turn once to grease surface. Let rise 1 hour or until double in size; punch dough down.

Divide dough in half. On lightly floured surface, roll half of dough to 12x8-inch rectangle. Spread half of butter over dough. Combine ½ cup sugar and cinnamon. Sprinkle half of sugar mixture over buttered surface. Starting from long side, roll in jelly roll fashion. Repeat with remaining dough, butter and sugar mixture. Place on greased baking sheet and let rise until double in size. Convection Bake at 325°F. for 35 to 40 minutes or until golden brown.

**Makes 2 French-style loaves**

*Evenly sprinkle sugar-cinnamon mixture over dough.*

*Starting from long side, roll in jelly roll fashion.*

▲ *Braided Egg Bread*

## *Braided Egg Bread*

**2 ½ cups all-purpose flour, divided**
**2 tablespoons sugar**
**1 ( ¼ oz.) pkg. dry yeast**
**¼ teaspoon salt**
**⅔ cup warm water**
**2 tablespoons butter**
**1 egg, beaten**

In large mixer bowl, combine 1 ½ cups flour, sugar, yeast, salt, water, butter and egg. Beat with electric mixer on medium speed for 2 minutes. Stir in remaining flour to form soft dough. Cover; let rise about 1 hour or until double in size. Roll dough out on lightly floured surface into 12x6-inch rectangle. Cut into 3 long pieces 12x2-inch each. Roll each piece into a strand. On lightly greased baking sheet, braid the three strands together to make a loaf. Cover; let rise about 1 hour or until double in size. Convection Bake at 375°F. for 13 to 16 minutes.

**Makes 1 French-style loaf**

## Basic White Bread

5 ¾ to 6 ¼ cups all-
   purpose flour, divided
2 (¼ oz.) pkgs. dry yeast
2 ¼ cups milk
3 tablespoons sugar
3 tablespoons vegetable
   shortening
2 teaspoons salt

In large mixer bowl, combine 2 ½ cups flour and yeast. In saucepan, heat and stir milk, sugar, shortening and salt until warm (120° to 130°) and shortening is nearly melted. Add to flour mixture. Beat with electric mixer on low speed for 30 seconds, scraping bowl constantly. Beat on high speed for 3 minutes. With a spoon, stir in as much of remaining flour as possible.

Turn out dough onto lightly floured surface. Knead in enough of remaining flour to make a moderately stiff dough that is smooth and elastic (6 to 8 minutes). Shape into a ball. Place in a lightly greased bowl; turn once to grease surface. Cover; let rise until double in size.

Punch dough down. Turn out onto lightly floured surface. Divide dough in half. Cover; let rest 10 minutes. Shape each half into a loaf. Place shaped dough in two lightly greased 8x4x2-inch loaf pans. Cover; let rise until nearly double in size (30 to 40 minutes). Place offset oven rack on bottom (A) shelf position. Convection Bake at 325°F. for 30 to 35 minutes or until done. Remove from pans immediately. Cool on wire racks.

**Makes 2 loaves**

## Dilly-Onion Bread

1 (¼ oz.) pkg. dry yeast
¼ cup warm water
1 cup small curd
   cottage cheese,
   room temperature
1 egg, beaten
2 tablespoons sugar
2 tablespoons dill seed
1 teaspoon celery seed
1 tablespoon dried onions
2 ¼ cups all-purpose flour
1 teaspoon salt
¼ teaspoon baking soda
2 tablespoons butter,
   melted

In large mixing bowl, sprinkle yeast over warm water; stir to dissolve. Mix in cottage cheese, egg, sugar, dill seed, celery seed and dried onions. Sift together flour, salt and baking soda. Add to cottage cheese mixture; stir well. Cover. Let rise, in warm place, 1 hour or until double in size. Stir dough down and pour into well-buttered 8-inch souffle dish. Cover. Let rise about 45 minutes or until nearly double in size. Convection Bake at 325°F. for 35 to 40 minutes or until browned. Brush with melted butter and cool on wire rack.

**Makes 1 round loaf**

## Buttery Batter Bread

1 cup warm milk (110°F.)
¾ cup butter, melted
¼ cup sugar
1 ½ teaspoons salt
1 (¼ oz.) pkg. dry yeast
4 cups all-purpose flour,
   divided
4 eggs, slightly beaten

In large mixer bowl, combine milk, butter, sugar and salt. Add yeast; stir to dissolve.

Add 2 cups flour and eggs. Beat with an electric mixer at medium speed 2 minutes until smooth. Stir in remaining 2 cups flour. Let rise 1 hour. Stir down and pour into well-greased, 10-inch tube pan. Cover; let rise about 45 minutes or until double in size. Convection Bake at 350°F. for 30 to 35 minutes.

**Makes 1 loaf**

# Desserts

▲ *Peach Torte*

## Peach Torte

**3 tablespoons butter**
**½ cup brown sugar,**
**   firmly packed**
**1 egg**
**1 teaspoon vanilla**
**¾ cup all-purpose flour**
**¼ teaspoon baking soda**
**¼ teaspoon salt**
**½ cup milk**
**½ cup graham cracker**
**   crumbs**
**⅓ cup pecans, chopped**
**1 cup fresh peaches,**
**   peeled and sliced**
**Pineapple juice**
**1 cup whipping cream**

Grease bottom of 8-inch round cake pan and line with wax paper. In medium mixing bowl, cream butter and brown sugar with an electric mixer until light and fluffy. Add egg and vanilla. Stir well to blend. Gradually blend in flour, baking soda, salt and milk. Fold in cracker crumbs and pecans. Spread batter into pan. Convection Bake at 325°F. for 25 to 30 minutes. Cool on wire rack for 5 minutes. Invert onto wire rack and remove wax paper. Cool 10 minutes. Split cake into 2 layers. Brush fresh peaches with pineapple juice; set aside.

In small mixing bowl, beat whipping cream with an electric mixer until soft peaks form. Spread one-half of whipped cream on bottom layer and top with peach slices, reserving enough peach slices to garnish the top. Add remaining cake layer. Spread remaining whipped cream over top of cake and garnish with reserved peaches. Chill 2 hours.

**Makes 6 to 8 servings**

## Pecan Cream Roll

**4 eggs, separated**
**1½ teaspoons vanilla**
**Dash salt**
**½ cup granulated sugar**
**¼ cup all-purpose flour, sifted**
**¾ cup pecans, finely chopped**
**Powdered sugar**

**Filling:**
**2 cups whipping cream**
**½ cup granulated sugar**

In medium mixing bowl, beat egg whites, vanilla and salt with an electric mixer until soft peaks form. Gradually add granulated sugar, beating until stiff peaks form. Beat egg yolks until thick and lemon colored. Fold beaten egg yolks into whites. Carefully fold in flour and pecans. Spread batter evenly into greased and floured 15x10x1-inch jelly roll pan. Convection Bake at 350°F. for 9 to 11 minutes. Immediately loosen sides and turn out onto towel sprinkled with powdered sugar. Starting at narrow end, roll cake and towel together; cool on wire rack. In medium mixing bowl, beat whipping cream until soft peaks form. Add granulated sugar and continue beating until firm. Unroll cake and spread with ¾ of filling. Roll cake and use remaining filling to decorate top; chill.

**Makes 8 servings**

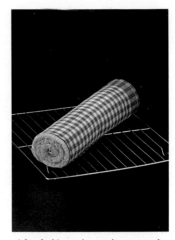

*After baking, place cake on towel and roll together.*

## Caramel Bundt Cake

**1 (18 oz.) box yellow cake mix**
**⅓ cup creamy peanut butter**
**4 eggs**
**¾ cup water**
**⅓ cup vegetable oil**
**¼ teaspoon vanilla**
**1 cup unsalted peanuts, chopped**
**1 cup (6 oz.) semisweet chocolate chips**

In large mixing bowl, combine cake mix, peanut butter, eggs, water, oil and vanilla. Beat on medium speed for 3 minutes with an electric mixer. Pour one-third of the cake batter into greased and floured 12-cup Bundt pan; sprinkle one-third cup peanuts and one-third cup chocolate chips over batter. Repeat with remaining batter, peanuts and chocolate chips. Convection Bake at 350°F. for 40 to 45 minutes. Cool on wire rack for 10 minutes before removing from pan. Top with Caramel Glaze (see below).

**Makes 8 to 10 servings**

*When cooled, unroll cake and spread with filling.*

**Caramel Glaze:**
**2 tablespoons butter, melted**
**¾ cup brown sugar, firmly packed**
**1 teaspoon cornstarch**
**½ teaspoon butter flavoring**
**¼ cup whipping cream**
**½ teaspoon vanilla**

In 4-cup glass measure, combine butter, brown sugar, cornstarch and butter flavoring. Mix until smooth. Gradually add whipping cream, stirring to blend. Microwave at HIGH (10) 2 to 3 minutes until thickened. Stir in vanilla. Cool to room temperature.

**Makes 1¼ cups**

# Desserts

▲ *Chocolate Cheesecake*

## Chocolate Cheesecake

1 ¼ cups chocolate wafer
    crumbs
¼ cup butter, melted
8 (1 oz.) squares semisweet
    chocolate,
    coarsely chopped
3 (8 oz.) pkgs. cream
    cheese, softened
1 cup sugar
3 eggs
2 tablespoons Kahlua
1 teaspoon vanilla
1 ½ cups sour cream
½ cup semisweet
    chocolate chips

In small mixing bowl, combine chocolate wafer crumbs and butter; stir well. Press crumb mixture into bottom and 1-inch up sides of 9-inch springform pan. Chill. In 4-cup glass measure, place chocolate squares. Microwave at HIGH (10) 2 to 3 minutes until melted. In medium mixing bowl, beat together cream cheese and sugar with an electric mixer until light and fluffy. Beat in eggs, melted chocolate, Kahlua and vanilla until smooth. Fold in sour cream. Pour mixture into crumb crust. Convection Bake at 325°F. for 1 hour to 1 hour 10 minutes or until center is nearly set. Turn oven off and let cheesecake stand in oven 30 minutes with oven door ajar. Remove and cool on wire rack. Cover and chill at least 8 hours. Garnish with chocolate leaves.

**To make chocolate leaves:** Microwave ½ cup semisweet chocolate chips at HIGH (10) ½ to 1 minute until melted. Brush chocolate on leaves. Chill until set. Carefully peel leaf away from chocolate.

**Makes one 9-inch cheesecake**

## Cream Puffs

½ cup water
¼ cup butter
½ cup all-purpose flour
⅛ teaspoon salt
2 eggs

In medium saucepan, combine water and butter; bring to a boil. Remove from heat. Beat in flour and salt until dough forms a ball and leaves sides of pan. Add eggs, one at a time, beating after each addition until smooth. Drop batter in 6 mounds onto ungreased baking sheet. Convection Bake at 400°F. for 15 minutes. Puncture each puff twice with toothpick to release steam. Continue baking 5 to 8 minutes or until golden brown. Remove from baking sheet and cool on wire rack. Split puffs and remove any soft dough from inside. Fill with pudding or ice cream. Replace tops. Serve immediately.

**Makes 6 servings**

*To fill, slice off tops and spoon filling into center.*

## Favorite Cherry Pie

2 (16 oz.) cans pitted tart
    red cherries (water pack)
1 cup sugar
¼ cup cornstarch
½ teaspoon
    almond extract
⅛ teaspoon allspice
⅛ teaspoon nutmeg
1 tablespoon butter
6 drops red food coloring
Pastry for 2-crust
    (9-inch) pie

Drain cherries, reserving 1 cup liquid. In a large saucepan, combine reserved cherry liquid, sugar and cornstarch. Cook over medium heat until thickened and bubbly, stirring constantly. Cook and stir 2 minutes longer. Stir in drained cherries, almond extract, allspice, nutmeg, butter and food coloring. Cool.

Pour cherry mixture into pastry-lined pie plate. Top with lattice crust. Seal and flute edges. Convection Bake at 400°F. for 40 to 45 minutes or until golden brown.

**Makes 8 servings**

## Holiday Pumpkin Pie

½ cup brown sugar,
    firmly packed
½ cup all-purpose flour
¼ cup butter
¼ cup pecans,
    finely chopped
1 (16 oz.) can pumpkin
1 cup brown sugar,
    firmly packed
1 tablespoon pumpkin pie
    spice
1 tablespoon all-purpose
    flour
½ teaspoon salt
1 cup half & half
2 eggs, beaten
Pastry for 1-crust
    (9-inch) pie

Combine ½ cup brown sugar and flour; cut in butter until crumbly. Stir in nuts. Set aside.

In large mixing bowl blend together pumpkin, 1 cup brown sugar, pumpkin pie spice, flour, salt, half & half and eggs. Pour filling into pastry-lined pie plate. Convection Bake at 350°F. for 45 minutes. Sprinkle with brown sugar-nut mixture and continue baking 10 minutes or until knife inserted near center comes out clean.

**Makes 8 servings**

# Desserts

▲ Apple Pie

## Apple Pie

**2 lbs. baking apples,
      peeled and sliced
1 tablespoon lemon juice
¾ cup sugar
2 tablespoons all-purpose
      flour
1¼ teaspoons cinnamon
⅛ teaspoon nutmeg
⅛ teaspoon salt
¼ teaspoon almond
      extract
½ cup raisins
Butter
Pastry for 2-crust
      (9-inch) pie**

In large mixing bowl, toss sliced apples with lemon juice. In small mixing bowl, combine sugar, flour, cinnamon, nutmeg and salt; add to apples and toss until well coated. Add almond extract and raisins. Pour apple mixture into pastry-lined pie plate. Dot with butter. Top with remaining pastry and flute the edges. Slit top of pastry to vent. Convection Bake at 425°F. for 10 minutes. Reduce heat to 375°F. and continue baking 40 to 45 minutes or until golden brown.

**Makes 8 servings**

## Fruited Oatmeal Cookies

**¾ cup butter, softened
1¾ cups all-purpose flour
1 cup brown sugar,
      firmly packed
½ cup granulated sugar
1 teaspoon baking powder
½ teaspoon baking soda
½ teaspoon cinnamon
½ teaspoon nutmeg
1 egg
1 teaspoon vanilla
2 cups oats, uncooked
1 cup mixed dried
      fruit bits
½ cup nuts, chopped**

Preheat oven to 375°F.

In mixing bowl beat butter with an electric mixer on medium-high speed for 30 seconds. Add half of flour, brown sugar, granulated sugar, baking powder, baking soda, cinnamon, nutmeg, egg and vanilla. Beat until thoroughly combined. Beat in remaining flour. Stir in oats, fruit bits and nuts.

Drop by rounded teaspoons 2 inches apart onto an ungreased baking sheet. Convection Bake at 375°F. for 8 to 10 minutes or until edges are golden. (To use Multi-Shelf Baking feature, refer to page 8.) Cool cookies on wire rack.

**Makes about 4 dozen**

## Lemon Cooler Cookies

1 cup butter, softened
½ cup granulated sugar
1 tablespoon fresh
    lemon rind, grated
1 egg yolk
½ teaspoon lemon extract
½ teaspoon vanilla
2 ¼ cups all-purpose flour
Granulated sugar
Powdered sugar

Preheat oven to 350°F.
In medium mixing bowl, cream butter and granulated sugar with an electric mixer until light and fluffy. Beat in lemon rind, egg yolk, lemon extract and vanilla. Gradually add flour and beat until blended. Roll 1 tablespoon of dough to form ball. Place on ungreased baking sheet. Dip bottom of 2 ½-inch round glass into sugar. Using bottom of glass, flatten to ¼-inch thickness. Convection Bake at 350°F. for 9 to 12 minutes or until edges begin to brown. (To use Multi-Shelf Baking feature, refer to page 8.) Cool on wire rack. Sift powdered sugar over top.

**Makes about 3½ dozen**

*Use bottom of glass dipped in sugar to flatten cookies.*

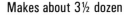

## Peanutty Chocolate Chip Cookies

1 cup butter, softened
1 cup brown sugar,
    firmly packed
½ cup granulated sugar
1⅓ cups (12 oz. jar)
    chunky peanut butter
1 egg
1½ teaspoons vanilla
1½ teaspoons butter
    flavoring
Dash salt
1½ cups all-purpose flour
2 cups (12 oz.) semisweet
    chocolate chips
1 cup dry roasted peanuts,
    chopped

Preheat oven to 325°F.
In medium mixing bowl, cream butter, brown sugar and granulated sugar with an electric mixer until fluffy. Add peanut butter, egg, vanilla, butter flavoring and salt and continue to mix with an electric mixer until well blended. Stir in flour, chocolate chips and peanuts. For each cookie, place 1 tablespoon of dough onto lightly greased baking sheet; flatten to ¼-inch thickness. Space cookies about ½-inch apart. Convection Bake at 325°F. for 12 to 14 minutes or until golden brown. (To use Multi-Shelf Baking feature, refer to page 8.) Let stand 3 minutes. Remove to wire rack to cool.

**Makes about 3 dozen**

## White Chocolate Fudge Brownies

1 cup (6 oz.) semisweet
    chocolate chips
⅔ cup sugar
½ cup butter, softened
2 large eggs
1 teaspoon vanilla
½ cup all-purpose flour
½ teaspoon baking
    powder
½ teaspoon salt
6 oz. white chocolate,
    chopped

Grease an 8-inch square baking pan. In food processor, place chocolate chips and sugar. Cover. Process until chocolate is as fine as sugar. Add butter, eggs and vanilla and mix for 1 minute. Blend in flour, baking powder, salt and white chocolate. Place batter in prepared pan. Convection Bake at 350°F. for 40 to 45 minutes or until toothpick inserted in center comes out clean.

**Makes about 3 dozen (1½-inch) squares**

*Combine chocolate and sugar and process until chocolate is as fine as sugar.*

## Convection Baking Chart

1. As a general rule, reduce conventional baking temperatures by 25°F. when converting recipes for the convection oven.
2. Frozen and refrigerated convenience foods should be baked according to package directions unless otherwise indicated in the chart below.
3. Shiny aluminum utensils give best results. However, all the utensils normally used for conventional baking will perform well in the convection oven.
4. Preheating the oven is usually not necessary. However, preheating may be desirable for foods with short cook times, such as cookies and biscuits.
5. Allow ample space between and around pans for proper circulation of heated air.
6. Keep oven door openings to a minimum while food is cooking.

| FOOD | | Oven Temp. | Time, Min. | Comments |
|---|---|---|---|---|
| **Breads** | Biscuits | 425° | 12 to 15 | Use Multi-Shelf feature for baking more than 1 sheet of biscuits. |
| | Corn Bread | 400° | 15 to 20 | |
| | Muffins | 375° | 12 to 16 | Remove from pans immediately and cool slightly on wire rack. |
| | Popovers | 375° | 35 to 40 | Prick each popover with a fork after removing from oven to allow steam to escape. |
| | Nut Bread or Fruit Bread | 325° | 40 to 60 | Interiors will be moist and tender. |
| | Yeast Bread | 325° | 30 to 35 | Use offset rack in bottom (A) shelf position. |
| | Plain or Sweet Rolls | 350° | 13 to 16 | Lightly grease baking sheet. |
| **Cakes** | Angel Food | 350° | 30 to 35 | Invert and cool in pan. |
| | Cheesecake | 325° | 65 to 70 | After cooking, turn oven off and let cheesecake stand in oven 30 minutes with door ajar. |
| | Coffee Cake | 350° | 25 to 30 | |
| | Cup Cakes | 300° | 20 to 25 | Use Multi-Shelf feature for baking more than one pan. |
| | Fruit Cake (loaf) | 275° | 80 to 90 | Interior will be moist and tender. |
| | Gingerbread | 325° | 35 to 40 | |
| | Jelly Roll | 350° | 9 to 12 | |
| | Butter Cakes (2 layers) | 300° | 30 to 40 | Use third (C) shelf position. |
| | Cake Mixes (2 layers) | 300° | 30 to 40 | Use third (C) shelf position. |
| | Fluted Tube Cake | 350° | 40 to 45 | Grease and flour pan. |
| | Pound Cake | 300° | 55 to 65 | Cool in pan 10 minutes before inverting on wire rack. |
| **Cookies** | Bar | 350° | 35 to 45 | |
| | Drop or Sliced | 325° | 12 to 14 | Use Multi-Shelf feature. Preheating the oven may be necessary. |

## Convection Baking Chart  *continued*

| FOOD | | Oven Temp. | Time, Min. | Comments |
|---|---|---|---|---|
| **Fruits, Other Desserts** | Baked Apples or Pears | 350° | 30 to 40 | Bake in utensil with shallow sides. |
| | Bread Pudding | 300° | 35 to 40 | Pudding is done when knife inserted near center comes out clean. |
| | Cream Puffs | 400° | 20 to 23 | Puncture puffs twice with toothpick to release steam after 15 minutes of baking time. |
| | Custard (individual) | 300° | 35 to 40 | Set cups in baking dish. Pour boiling water around cups to a depth of 1 inch. |
| | Fruit Compote | 325° | 30 to 35 | |
| | Meringue Shells | 275° | 30 to 35 | When done, turn oven off and let shells stand in oven 1 hour to dry. |
| **Pies, Pastries** | Frozen | 375° | 40 to 45 | Follow procedure on package. |
| | Meringue-topped | 325° | 13 to 16 | |
| | Two-crust | 400° to 425° | 45 to 55 | |
| | Quiche | 325° | 35 to 50 | Let stand 10 minutes before cutting. |
| | Pastry Shell | 425° | 10 to 16 | Prick pastry with fork to prevent shrinkage. |
| **Casseroles** | Meat, chicken, seafood combinations | 325° to 350° | 20 to 40 | Cook times vary with casserole size and ingredients. |
| | Pasta | 325° to 350° | 25 to 45 | Cook times vary with casserole size and ingredients. |
| | Potatoes, scalloped | 325° | 55 to 60 | Let stand 5 minutes before serving. |
| | Vegetable | 325° to 350° | 25 to 35 | Cook times vary with casserole size and ingredients. |
| **Convenience Foods** | Frozen Bread Dough | 325° | 30 to 35 | Use offset rack in bottom (A) shelf position. |
| | Frozen Dinners | 350° | 20 to 25 | Follow package directions. |
| | Frozen Entrees | 350° | 50 to 60 | Follow package directions. |
| | Frozen Pizza Rolls, Egg Rolls | 400° | 8 to 10 | Follow package directions. |
| | Pizza | 375° | 20 to 22 | |
| | Slice and Bake Cookies | 325° | 8 to 12 | Preheating the oven may be necessary. Let stand a few minutes on baking sheet before removing to cool. |
| **Main Dishes** | Meat Loaf | 325° | 55 to 60 | |
| | Oven-baked Stew | 325° | 80 to 90 | Brown meat before combining with liquid and vegetables. |
| | Swiss Steak | 325° | 55 to 60 | |
| | Stuffed Peppers | 325° | 40 to 45 | Use green, red or yellow peppers. |
| **Vegetables** | Acorn Squash | 325° | 50 to 60 | Turn squash halves cut side up after 30 minutes of cook time. |
| | Baked Potatoes | 400° | 45 to 50 | Prick skins with a fork before baking. |
| | Twice-Baked Potatoes | 400° | 20 to 25 | |

# Convection Roasting Chart

| MEATS | | Minutes / Lb. | Oven Temp. | Internal Temp. |
|---|---|---|---|---|
| **Beef** | Rib (3 to 5 lbs.) | | | |
| | Rare | 20 to 24 | 325° | 140° |
| | Medium | 24 to 28 | 325° | 160° |
| | Well | 28 to 32 | 325° | 170° |
| | Boneless Rib, Top Sirloin | | | |
| | Rare | 20 to 24 | 325° | 140° |
| | Medium | 24 to 28 | 325° | 160° |
| | Well | 28 to 32 | 325° | 170° |
| | Beef Tenderloin | | | |
| | Rare | 10 to 14 | 325° | 140° |
| | Medium | 14 to 18 | 325° | 160° |
| | Pot Roast (2½ to 3 lbs.) | | | |
| | Chuck, Rump | 35 to 45 | 300° | 170° |
| **Pork** | Bone-in (3 to 5 lbs.) | 23 to 27 | 325° | 170° |
| | Boneless (3 to 5 lbs.) | 23 to 27 | 325° | 170° |
| | Pork Chops (½ to 1-inch thick) | | | |
| | 2 chops | 30 to 35 total | 325° | 170° |
| | 4 chops | 35 to 40 total | 325° | 170° |
| | 6 chops | 40 to 45 total | 325° | 170° |
| **Ham** | Canned (3 lb. fully cooked) | 14 to 18 | 325° | 140° |
| | Butt (5 lb. fully cooked) | 14 to 18 | 325° | 140° |
| | Shank (5 lb. fully cooked) | 14 to 18 | 325° | 140° |
| **Lamb** | Bone-in (3 to 5 lbs.) | | | |
| | Medium | 17 to 20 | 325° | 160° |
| | Well | 20 to 24 | 325° | 170° |
| | Boneless (3 to 5 lbs.) | | | |
| | Medium | 17 to 20 | 325° | 160° |
| | Well | 20 to 24 | 325° | 170° |
| **Seafood** | Fish, whole (3 to 5 lbs.) | 30 to 40 total | 400° | |
| | Lobster Tails (6 to 8 oz. each) | 20 to 25 total | 350° | |
| **Poultry** | Whole Chicken (2½ to 3½ lbs.) | 24 to 26 | 350° | 180° to 185° |
| | Cornish Hens | | | |
| | Unstuffed (1 to 1½ lbs.) | 50 to 55 total | 350° | 180° to 185° |
| | Stuffed (1 to 1½ lbs.) | 55 to 60 total | 350° | 180° to 185° |
| | Duckling (4 to 5 lbs.) | 24 to 26 | 325° | 180° to 185° |
| | Turkey, whole* | | | |
| | Unstuffed (10 to 16 lbs.) | 8 to 11 | 325° | 180° to 185° |
| | Unstuffed (18 to 24 lbs.) | 7 to 10 | 325° | 180° to 185° |
| | Turkey Breast (4 to 6 lbs.) | 16 to 19 | 325° | 170° |

*Stuffed birds generally require 30 to 45 minutes additional roasting time. Shield legs and breast with foil to prevent over browning and drying of skin.

## Broiling Chart

1. Always use broiler pan and rack that comes with the oven. It is designed to minimize smoking and spattering by trapping juices in the shielded lower part of the pan.
2. Slash fat evenly around outside edges of steaks and chops to prevent curling during broiling. Use tongs when turning meat to prevent piercing meat and loosing juices.
3. If desired, marinate meats or chicken before broiling. Brush with sauce or marinade during last 5 minutes only.

| FOOD | | Quantity and/or Thickness | Broil Setting | First Side Time, Min. | Second Side Time, Min. | Comments |
|---|---|---|---|---|---|---|
| Bacon | | ½ lb. (about 8 thin slices) | HI | 5 | 2 to 3 | Arrange in single layer. |
| Ground Beef | Well done | 1 lb. (4 ¼-lb. patties) | HI | 7 | 4 to 5 | Space evenly on pan. |
| Beef Steaks, Tender Cuts | T-bone, rib-eye, filet mignon, loin or strip, etc. | 1-in. thick | | Rare: 6<br>Medium: 7<br>Well Done: 9 | 4 to 6<br>5 to 7<br>7 to 10 | Steaks less than 1-in. thick cook through before browning. Cook first side just to turn meat color then finish other side to desired doneness. |
| | | 1½-in. thick | | Rare: 7<br>Medium: 8<br>Well Done: 11 | 5 to 7<br>6 to 8<br>8 to 11 | Slash fat. |
| Chicken pieces | | (2½ to 3 lbs.) | LO | 16 | 12 to 14 | Chicken should be about 8 inches from heat. |
| Fish | Fish Steaks | ¾ to 1-in. thick | LO | 6 | 5 to 7 | Lightly grease rack of broil pan. |
| Lobster tails | (6 to 8 oz. each) | 2 to 4 | LO | 15 to 18 | Do not turn over | Brush with melted butter before and after half of time. |
| Ham slices | (precooked) | 1-in. thick | HI | 7 | 6 to 7 | |
| Pork chops | | 1-in. thick | HI | Well Done: 15 | 12 to 14 | Slash fat. |
| Lamb chops | | 1-in. thick<br>2 to 4 chops | HI | Medium: 6<br>Well Done: 8 | 5 to 6<br>8 to 10 | Slash fat. |
| | | 1½-in. thick<br>2 to 4 chops | HI | Medium: 11<br>Well Done: 14 | 11 to 13<br>14 to 16 | Slash fat. |
| Wieners | and similar precooked sausages or bratwurst | 1 lb. | HI | 4 | 2 to 4 | If desired, split sausages in half lengthwise. |

# Index

# Index

*CREDITS:*
Wendy Shafer Shirrell, Editor
Manager, Consumer Information
  Testing Laboratory
GE Appliances

Design, Production, Photography
and Food Styling:
OTT Communications, Inc.
Louisville, Kentucky